Volume 3B

STEP BY STEP

An Introduction to Successful Practice

by Kerstin Wartberg

Exercise Book for Young Violinists and Their Parents
Based on the Mother-Tongue Method,
with Accompanying Audio

Translation from the German Edition "Schritt für Schritt" by Mike Hoover

Accompanying Play-Along Recording

Rudolf Gähler, Violin
Kerstin Wartberg, Violin
Kathrin Averdung, Violin

David Andruss, Piano
and
Piano arrangements for all recorded pieces
Ingo Klatt, Sound Engineer

Recorded in the Steinway-Haus Heinersdorff, Düsseldorf, Germany

Photography: German Suzuki Institute, Gudrun Søe Hansen, and Joachim Preuss

Stream or download the audio content for this book.
To access, visit: **alfred.com/redeem**
Enter the following code: 00-28084-560418

© 2007 Summy-Birchard Music, division of Summy-Birchard, Inc.
Exclusive print rights administered by Alfred Music
All rights reserved. Printed in USA.

ISBN-10: 0-7390-4771-X
ISBN-13: 978-0-7390-4771-2

Summy-Birchard Inc., exclusively administered by
Alfred Music

Any duplication, adaptation or arrangement of the compositions
contained in this collection requires the written consent of the Publisher.
No part of this book may be photocopied or reproduced in any way without permission.
Unauthorized uses are an infringement of the U.S. Copyright Act and are punishable by law.

Foreword

How wondrous is the life force! One feels it everywhere. Through it we can enjoy the beauty of nature. Tiny buds become magical flowers, every morning the birds begin to sing, and countless leaves, grasses, and flowers herald to us the great life force. In addition to the magnificence of nature, we have also been given the gift of music. Music is the language of the spirit and should purify us and open our hearts for the sublime. We need to recognize that this gift is to be used. Sixty years ago, when I recognized the scope and mighty power of nature's developmental principles and realized that every child in the world learns his mother tongue without difficulty, I changed the outlook on my life and made countless discoveries. We should all learn to be an integral part of creation and not to oppose the life force. Once this is learned, we can reach unbelievable heights.

Our task as parents and teachers is to raise our children to be worthy people who will be able to assume responsibility for the further development of the world. Much is to be done. With courage, enterprise, and gratitude for the life force that is given to us, we can travel this road together.

Kerstin Wartberg was the first German to study at and graduate from the Talent Education Institute in Matsumoto, Japan. In the many years since then, my wife and I have been in close contact with her.

I am pleased that she wants to share my teaching method and philosophy with the interested reader. I wish her publication a large circulation and hope that it falls on fertile ground.

Dr. Shinichi Suzuki
with his wife Waltraud and Kerstin Wartberg

Matsumoto, June 1994

Shinichi Suzuki

Contents for this Book and the Companion Audio

Introduction: *Dear Parents! Dear Colleagues!* — Pages 6-7

- ⊙ 1   The Tuning Notes A – D – G – E   (A = 441 Hertz)

I. Warm-Up Exercises — Pages 8-17

⊙ 2	English Canon	(Three Violins and Piano)
⊙ 3	The Bell Song in G Major (3rd position)	(Piano Accompaniment)
⊙ 4	The Bell Song in G Minor (3rd position)	(Piano Accompaniment)
⊙ 5	The Bell Song in C Major (3rd position)	(Piano Accompaniment)
⊙ 6	The Bell Song in C Minor (3rd position)	(Piano Accompaniment)
⊙ 7	Marionette Dance, E string (2nd position)	(Violin and Piano)
⊙ 8	Marionette Dance, A string (2nd position)	(Piano Accompaniment)
⊙ 9	Marionette Dance, D string (2nd position)	(Piano Accompaniment)
⊙ 10	Marionette Dance, G string (2nd position)	(Piano Accompaniment)
⊙ 11	Climbing Melody 1 (Scales)	(Violin and Piano)
⊙ 12	Climbing Melody 2 (Arpeggios)	(Violin and Piano)
⊙ 13	Nightingale (Trill Exercise)	(Nightingale, Violin and Piano)
⊙ 14	Second Fall Melody (Exercise with Fourths)	(Violin and Piano)
	Snake Scale (Chromatic Exercise)	
	Bow exercises across two strings	
	Bow exercises across three strings	

II. Pieces, Songs and Exercises — Pages 18-46

Gavotte, *Jean Becker* — Pages 18-27

⊙ 15	Gavotte - in performance tempo	(Violin and Piano)
⊙ 16-18	Gavotte - in a slow practice tempo	(Violin and Piano)
⊙ 19	Gavotte - in a slow practice tempo	(Violin and Piano)
⊙ 20-22	Gavotte - in performance tempo	(Piano Accompaniment)
⊙ 23	Hej! Haj! - Hungarian Dance	(Violin and Piano)
⊙ 24	Double Stops Are So Much Fun	(Violin and Piano)

Gavotte I and II, *Johann Sebastian Bach* — Pages 28-35

⊙ 25	Gavotte I and II - in performance tempo	(Violin and Piano)
⊙ 26	Gavotte I, 1st section - in a slow practice tempo	(Violin and Piano)
⊙ 27	Gavotte I, 2nd section - in a slow practice tempo	(Violin and Piano)
⊙ 28	Gavotte II, 1st section - in a slow practice tempo	(Violin and Piano)
⊙ 29	Gavotte II, 2nd section - in a slow practice tempo	(Violin and Piano)
⊙ 30-31	Gavotte I and II - in a medium practice tempo	(Piano Accompaniment)
⊙ 32-33	Gavotte I and II - in performance tempo	(Piano Accompaniment)

Paganini Motion, *Kerstin Wartberg* — Pages 36-37

⊙ 34-36	Paganini Motion - in a medium practice tempo	(Violin and Piano)
⊙ 37-39	Paganini Motion - in performance tempo	(Violin and Piano)
⊙ 40-42	Paganini Motion - in performance tempo	(Piano Accompaniment)

Bourrée, *Johann Sebastian Bach* — Pages 38-46

⊙ 43	Bourrée - in performance tempo	(Violin and Piano)
⊙ 44	Bourrée, 1st section - in a slow practice tempo	(Violin and Piano)
⊙ 45	Bourrée, 2nd section - in a slow practice tempo	(Violin and Piano)
⊙ 46	Bourrée, 3rd section - in a slow practice tempo	(Violin and Piano)
⊙ 47	Bourrée, 4th section - in a slow practice tempo	(Violin and Piano)
⊙ 48-51	Bourrée - in a medium practice tempo	(Piano Accompaniment)
⊙ 52-55	Bourrée - in performance tempo	(Piano Accompaniment)

Some Original Movements for Violoncello Solo and Violin Solo by *Johann Sebastian Bach*

⊙ 56	From the Suite No. 3 for Violoncello Solo Bourrée I and II BWV 1009	Soloist: Michael Bach
⊙ 57	From the Partita in E-Major for Violin Solo Gavotte en Rondeau BWV 1006	Soloist: Rudolf Gähler
⊙ 58	From the Partita in E-Major for Violin Solo Preludio BWV 1006	Soloist: Rudolf Gähler

III. Appendix — Pages 47-60

Other Transcriptions of the Movements by *Johann Sebastian Bach*

Gavotte I and II — Pages 48-50
Bourrée — Pages 51-53

A Journey Back in Time to the World of Johann Sebastian Bach — Pages 54-59

Childhood Filled with Happiness and Sorrow (1685-1700)
Composers in Bach's Lifetime
The Clothing of the Nobles
Original Compositions and Arrangements in Baroque Music
Johann Sebastian Bach's Family Crest: Hidden Initials
A House Filled with Music (1723-1750)
My Musical Farewell

Graduation Certificate, Elementary Level — Page 60

🔔 = SYMBOL for additional Warm-Up Exercises

Illustrations

Portrait by Elias Gottlob Haussmann: Johann Sebastian Bach in 1748

Facsimile of *Bourrée from the Suite No. 3 for Violoncello Solo*:
hand copy by Anna Magdalena Bach

Autograph of *Preludio from the Partita in E-Major for Violin Solo*:
National Library of Berlin

Drawings: Eugenie Kok

Photographs: German Suzuki Institute

References

Malcolm Boyd: *Bach*, Schirmer 1983, 1997

From the first biography (1802) about Bach:
Johann Nikolaus Forkel: *Über Johann Sebastian Bachs Leben, Kunst und Kunstwerke*, newly released by Jos. Müller-Blattau, Bärenreiter-Verlag, Kassel 2004

Albert Schweitzer: *Johann Sebastian Bach*, Breitkopf & Härtel, Wiesbaden 1990

Dear Parents, Dear Colleagues!

In Book 3B we will complete the students' elementary level of violin training and, at the same time, prepare them for the intermediate level, which begins in Book 4. The concerto movements by Seitz, Vivaldi and Bach included in Book 4 will be considerably more demanding than any of the literature learned thus far.

Thematic Emphasis: Technical Preparation for the Intermediate Level

The warm-up exercises in Book 3B, together with the piece *Paganini Motion*, already present the most essential technical elements necessary for Suzuki Book 4. For the student, careful acquisition of these skills should be a top priority. In contrast to earlier books, a practice plan has not been included in this book. In its place you will find a graduation certificate listing thirteen fundamental exercises and *Paganini Motion*. Taking individual potentials into account, each of these exercises should be continually refined until they can be played at an exceptionally high level. Mastery of an exercise should then be documented on the certificate, which will allow students to see at a glance how they are progressing towards the intermediate level.

Thematic Emphasis: Johann Sebastian Bach

Musically, we want to occupy ourselves in detail with the composer Johann Sebastian Bach. He is the most frequently encountered composer in the series *Step by Step* and the *Suzuki Violin School*, appearing in most of the books, and consequently at each developmental level. The following table presents a brief summary of the included works of J.S. Bach, along with a bibliography of their original sources.

Johann Sebastian Bach

Book 1B
- Minuet 1: From the *Suite in G Minor for piano*, BWV 822
- Minuet 2: From the *Notebook for Anna Magdalena Bach*, BWV Anh. 116 (in G Major for harpsichord)
- Minuet 3: From the *Notebook for Anna Magdalena Bach*, BWV Anh. 114 (in G Major for piano)

Book 2A
- Musette: From the *English Suite No. 3*, BWV 808 (in G Minor for piano)

Books 3A and 3B
- Minuet I and II: From the *Notebook for Anna Magdalena Bach*, BWV Anh. 114/115 (for piano)
- Gavotte in G Minor: From the *Suite in G Minor for piano*, BWV 822
- Gavotte I and II: From the *Orchestra Suite No. 3 in D Major*, BWV 1068
- Bourrée: From the *Suite for Violoncello No. 3*, BWV 1009

Books 4 through 8
- Vivace: From the *Concerto for Two Violins and String Orchestra in D Minor*, BWV 1043
- Gavotte I and II: From the *Suite for Violoncello No. 5 in C Major*, BWV 1011
- Gigue: From the *Suite for Violoncello No. 1 in G Major*, BWV 1007
- Courante: From the *Suite for Violoncello No. 1 in G Major*, BWV 1007
- *Violin Concerto in A Minor*, BWV 1041
- Andante: From the *Sonata in C Major for Violin Solo*, BWV 1005
- Allegro: From the *Sonata for Violin and Continuo*, BWV 1023

I am sure you will agree with me that the ultimate purpose of violin lessons should not simply be the mastery of individual pieces. The impressions that we acquire through exposure to music and an instrument are much more important. These impressions will accompany your child for a lifetime, cultivate character traits and motivation, impart practical experience, and above all, open an inner path to artistic and spiritual values. We are not dealing with a short-term influence of the moment, but rather a long-term sensitization of the child. Music carves a path "into the depths of the human heart" (*Robert Schumann*) without words or explanations and can bypass the intellect to find the most direct route.

Suzuki was convinced that children who listened to the music of Johann Sebastian Bach would absorb some of his character traits and feelings. During my studies with Dr. Suzuki in Matsumoto, Japan, he often spoke about this subject. A quote from my notes: "When children grow up with the music of Bach, their souls will be directly influenced by Bach's spirit with its strong personality, deep religious earnestness, desire for order, and noble character. The life forces of children sense the traits of a composer and absorb them to bring them to life in themselves. I am certain that every heart capable of feeling music will assimilate its special radiance and its clear message."

Presenting a vivid encounter with the composer Johann Sebastian Bach, the article *A Journey Back in Time to the World of Johann Sebastian Bach* will provide parents and students with anecdotes, challenging tasks and information about Bach and his personal circumstances. Students and parents should read this text together. Depending on the students' ages, the article is likely to raise many questions requiring explanation. While some students will only be able to complete the assignments with parental help, others may find them very easy. Group lessons are also an ideal forum for answering these questions, completing the assignments, or discussing particular aspects of Bach's life in more depth.

Parents and teachers can further encourage their children and students to develop an interest in the world of music by providing appropriate books and recordings, with portraits of composers created especially for young audiences. It might also be inspiring to listen to recordings of original versions of works by Bach, especially those pieces appearing in the Suzuki Violin School. (Please see the list above.) All students in Book 3B should listen to the Orchestral Suite No. 3 in D Major, BWV 1068. Specific questions concerning this piece are provided on page 31.

Many violinists and cellists consider Bach's solo works to be highlights of the literature for their instruments. In order to introduce children to this profound musical genre, Suzuki included a total of four movements from the Suites for Violoncello Solo in his teaching repertoire, which are technically easier for violin students than the solo works for violin. A short chamber concert with solo works for violoncello and violin concludes the CD accompanying this book.

> *The following pieces by Johann Sebastian Bach can be found in Book 3B*:
>
> *Gavotte I and II* (From the *Orchestral Suite No. 3 in D Major*, BWV 1068)
> 1. **The transcription** in our book is taken from the original Suzuki Violin School, Edition 1978. It is written for violin and piano.
> 2. **Another transcription** for violin and piano with different bowings can be found on pages 48 - 49.
>
> *Bourrée I and II* (From the *Suite No. 3 for Violoncello Solo*, BWV 1009)
> 1. **The transcription** in our book is taken from the original Suzuki Violin School, Edition 1978. It is an arrangement for violin and piano that has become almost as well-known as the original version for violoncello.
> 2. **Another transcription** for violin and piano is printed on pages 51 - 52.
>
> *The following pieces by Johann Sebastian Bach can be heard on the CD:*
> 1. *Gavotte I and II*, **transcription** for violin and piano (From the original Suzuki Violin School, Edition 1978).
> 2. *Bourrée I and II*, **transcription** for violin and piano (From the original Suzuki Violin School, Edition 1978).
> 3. *Bourrée I and II*, **original version** from the *Suite No. 3 for Violoncello Solo*, BWV 1009.
> 4. *Gavotte en Rondeau*, **original version** from the *Partita in E Major for Violin Solo*, BWV 1006.
> 5. *Preludio*, **original version** from the *Partita in E Major for Violin Solo*, BWV 1006.

Thematic Emphasis: Original Compositions and Arrangements in the Baroque Period

Many pieces which are especially popular among players and audiences can often be found in a variety of arrangements. In the Baroque Period, it was considered an honor for a composer when colleagues would make arrangements of his works. After the motto "All is permitted that pleases!", no less a personality than **J. S. Bach** made arrangements of half of the 12 Vivaldi concertos op. 3 (one for four violins, two for three violins and three for one violin) for piano, organ, and even four harpsichords with string orchestra.

He transposed some of these pieces into different keys, changed bass lines and harmonies, fashioned figures to be more virtuosic, and even added or deleted measures.

Bach's pupil, *Johann Friedrich Agricola*, wrote in the year 1775 that Bach often played his pieces for violin or violoncello solo on the clavichord (a forerunner of the piano) adding chordal accompaniments to the melody. (See **Johann Nikolaus Forkel**: From the first biography in 1802 about Bach, Bärenreiter-Verlag, Kassel 2004). So it is certainly not a stylistic offence to include the *Bourrée* from the *Suite No. 3 for Violoncello Solo* as an arrangement for violin and piano in this book. This is simply a continuation of Bach's own frequent practice and is reminiscent of his free spirit.

Arrangements in Instrumental Pedagogy

When students like a piece, they are willing to work more intensely on difficult passages and tackle challenging technical issues such as bow speed, string crossings, tempo and intonation. This is why arrangements can be such valuable additions to the lesson repertoire. Expecting students to polish etudes to the same high levels of mastery at this stage of development will usually exhaust their perseverance and enthusiasm rather quickly. In book 4A, etudes and other musical literature will begin to play an increasingly important role in the successful building of intermediate and advanced technique.

The Written Music as Foundation for Our Work

Although Suzuki frequently challenged teachers to act freely and creatively in their manner of teaching, he did want them to remain faithful to certain elements. One of these was adherence to the common repertoire used by Suzuki students throughout the world, which has enabled them to communicate in the common language of music for many years. This thought is further embodied in the homogeneity of the worldwide student and teacher training and has great merit. Nevertheless, movements for change have emerged and some Suzuki materials are coming on the market with alternative versions and different editions of some pieces.

In order to familiarize teachers using the *Step by Step* books with some of these changes, alternative versions of *Gavotte I and II* and *Bourrée* by J. S. Bach appear in the appendix of this book. Aside from being informative, this will help teachers prepare their students for workshops which might use these alternative versions.

Incidentally, there is yet a third version of *Bourrée* printed on page 46: This is a facsimile of the hand-written manuscript by Anna Magdalena Bach from the year 1727. Upon closer examination, it is easy to see that neither of the transcriptions mentioned above can claim to be an exact copy of the original, to say nothing of the fact that they have been transposed from the cello to the violin.

I am convinced that Johann Sebastian Bach, and Shinichi Suzuki as well, would have been extremely happy to hear children around the world playing these pieces **together, regardless of the arrangement.** Both would have placed primary emphasis on the quality and musicality of the performances. In the interest of our children and students, we should not lose sight of these goals.

Kerstin Wartberg

Warm-Up Exercises

Vibrato Exercise with Violin and Bow

You have already seen this picture in book 2B. Thus far, this exercise has been performed without the bow.

Now, you should bow the open G string with a powerful tone while waving with your left hand.

You will observe something entirely new: The left hand movements cause your tone to "wobble."

Do you hear how this tone is similar to vibrato?

Tone and Vibrato Exercises

⊙₂ **English Canon for three violins**

Begin by practicing this piece alone. Always use the entire bow for each bow stroke and try to vibrate occasionally with the second or third finger. Even if this is still very difficult, you should try to use at least a little bit of vibrato on the very last note. You are probably familiar with the old proverbs:

No pain, no gain! *or somewhat altered* **No practice, no vibrato!**

Practice makes perfect! *or* **Only those who practice can improve!**

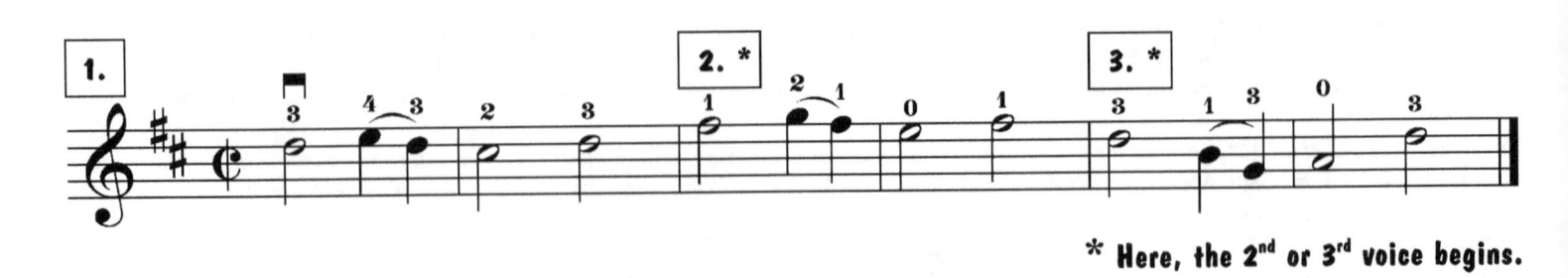

* Here, the 2ⁿᵈ or 3ʳᵈ voice begins.

Later, you can practice this peaceful canon in different ways:

- Each voice plays the canon through three times, beginning and ending at different times.

- The first voice plays the canon through three times with all voices ending together. This version can be heard on the CD.

- Each voice plays the first verse softly *(p)*, the second a bit louder *(mf)*, and the third very loud *(f)*.

The Bell Songs in Third Position

⊙₃ **The Bell Song in G Major**

⊙₄ **The Bell Song in G Minor**

⊙₅ **The Bell Song in C Major**

⊙₆ **The Bell Song in C Minor**

What do you need to consider when playing the Bell Songs in third position?

Write everything that you think is important in the following table!

1.	2.
3.	4.
5.	6.
7.	8.
9.	10.

Preparation for the Second Position

Shifting from first to second position with the first finger

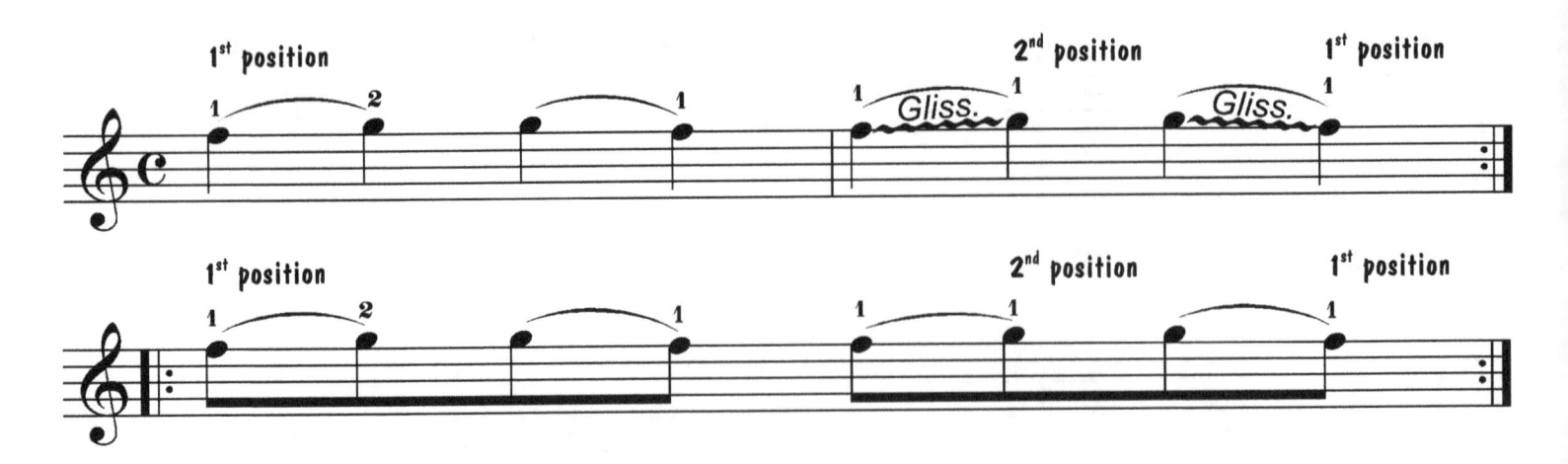

⊙₇ **Marionette Dance in 2nd Position, E string**

Begin by listening to Marionette Dance in 2nd Position and finger silently with the left hand.

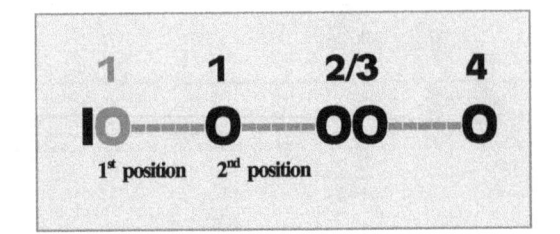

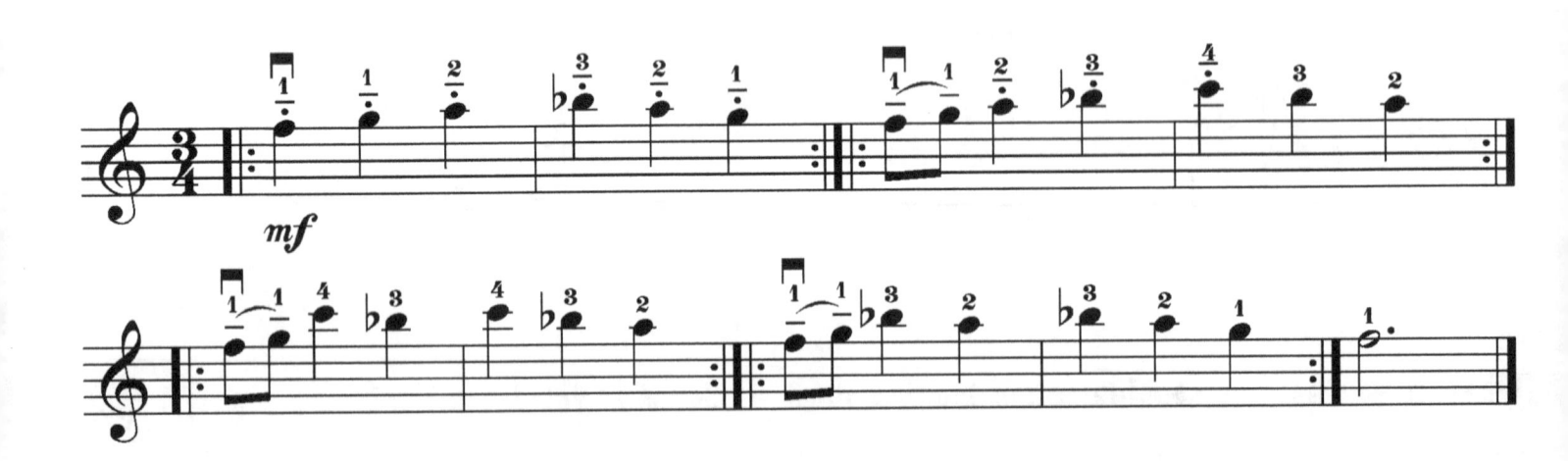

⊙₈ **Marionette Dance in 2nd Position, A string**

⊙₉ **Marionette Dance in 2nd Position, D string**

⊙₁₀ **Marionette Dance in 2nd Position, G string**

Climbing Melodies in 1ˢᵗ, 2ⁿᵈ and 3ʳᵈ Positions

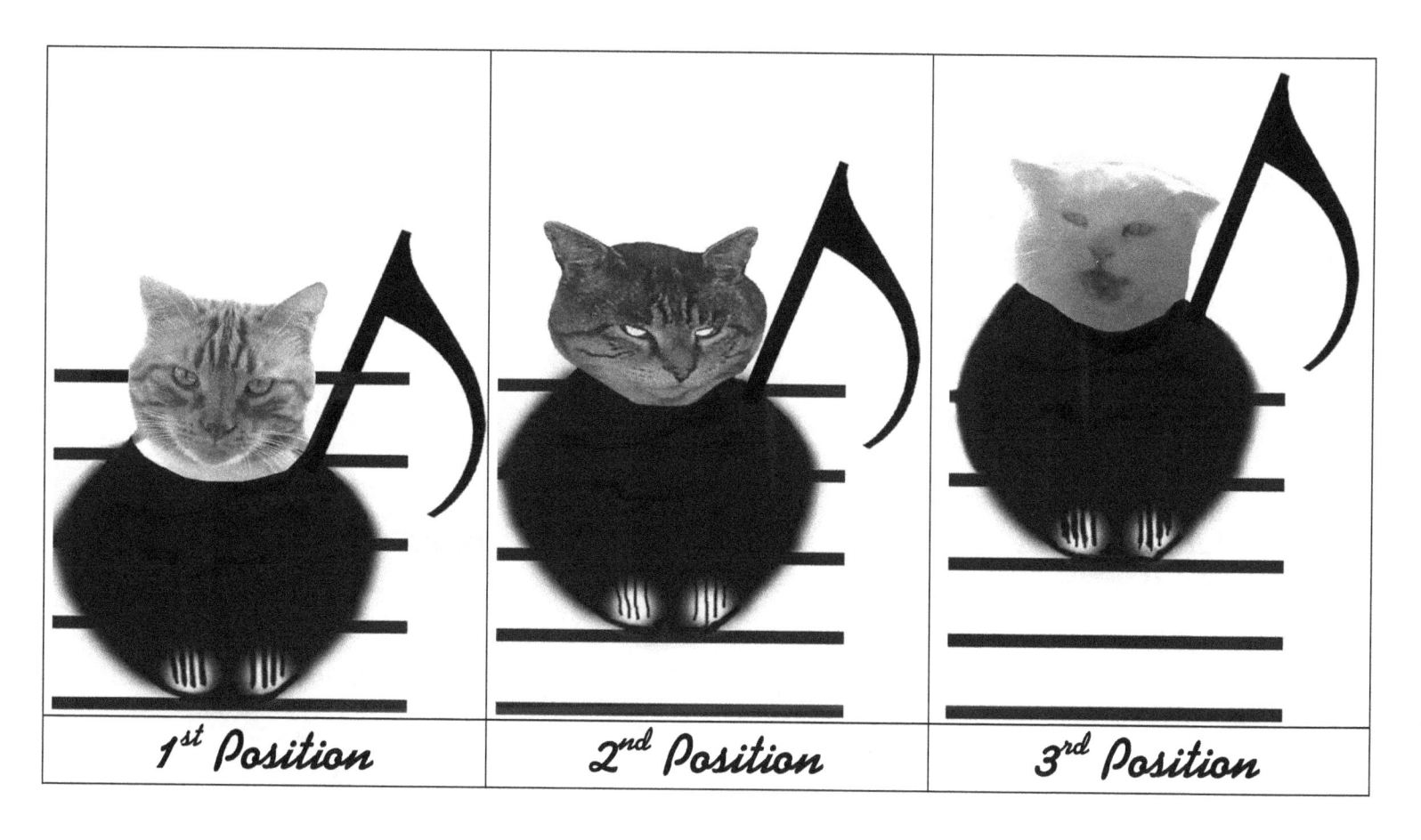

1ˢᵗ Position	2ⁿᵈ Position	3ʳᵈ Position

Scale Transpositions

What does this mean?

This is very simple! It means that you will play scales beginning on different notes. After each scale, you will climb one tone higher, changing to a new position, and then play a new scale beginning on the new note.

Now we want to practice this technique. You will quickly recognize that a single finger pattern will work for all of the following scales; in this case, the fourth finger pattern.

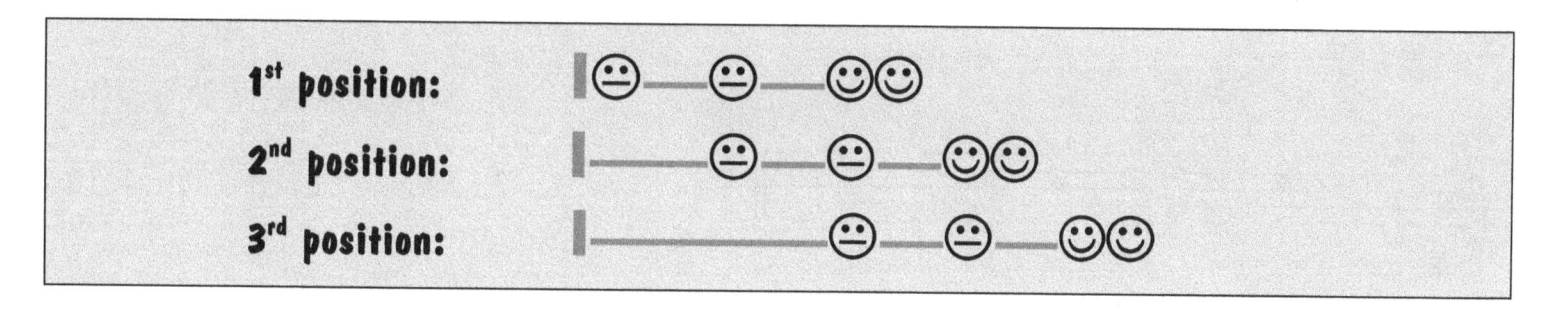

1ˢᵗ position:
2ⁿᵈ position:
3ʳᵈ position:

When you have mastered this method of transposition, the climbing melodies in different positions and keys will be very easy! The following exercises climb from the first to the second, and from the second to the third position. They change from B-flat to C major and end in D major.

Climbing Melody 1: Scales in the 1st, 2nd and 3rd Positions

The B-flat major scale in 1st position

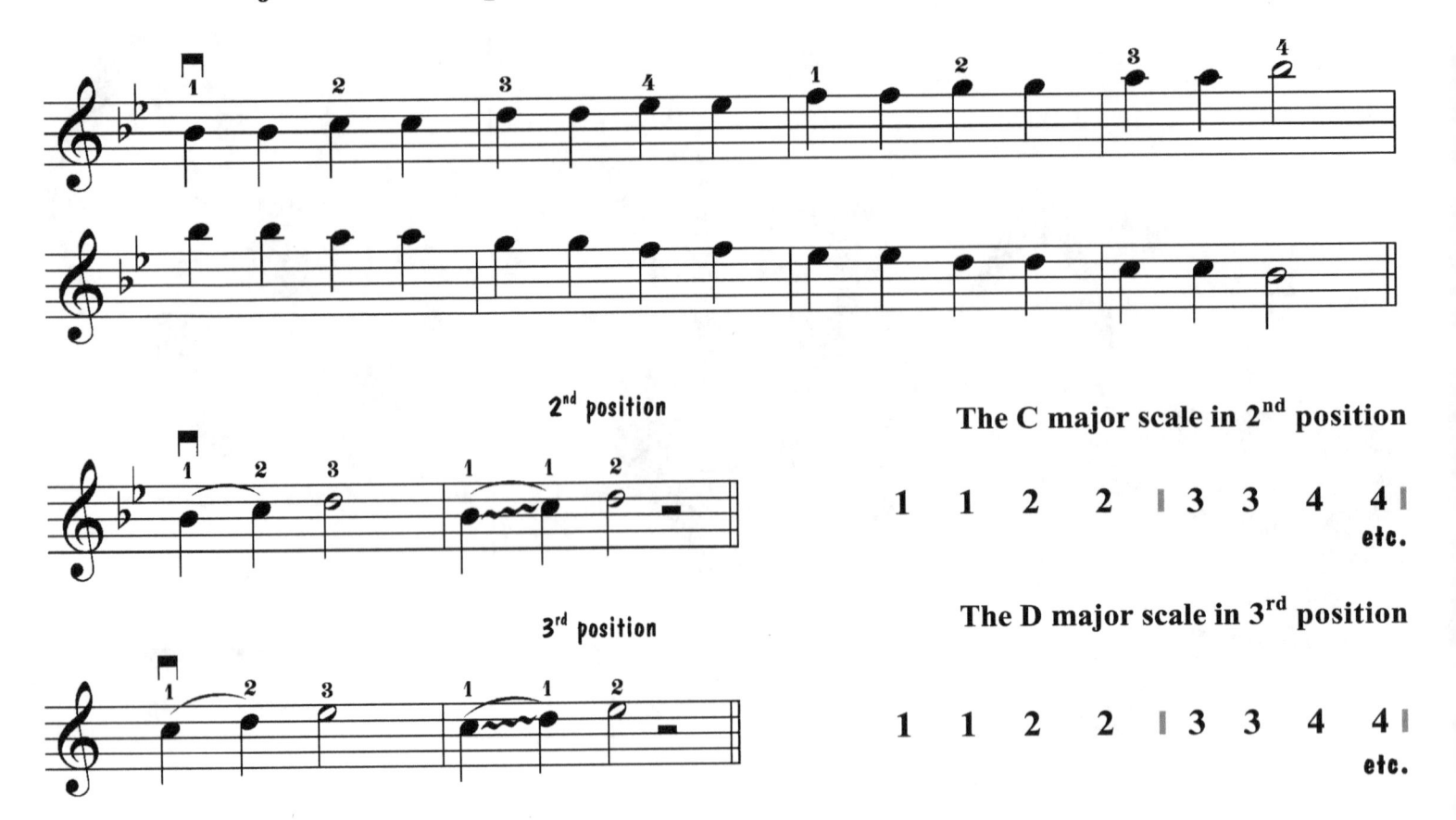

The C major scale in 2nd position

1   1   2   2 | 3   3   4   4 |
                              etc.

The D major scale in 3rd position

1   1   2   2 | 3   3   4   4 |
                              etc.

Climbing Melody 2: Arpeggios in the 1st, 2nd and 3rd Positions

For the following arpeggios you will also use only the fourth finger pattern.

Arpeggios in the 1st position

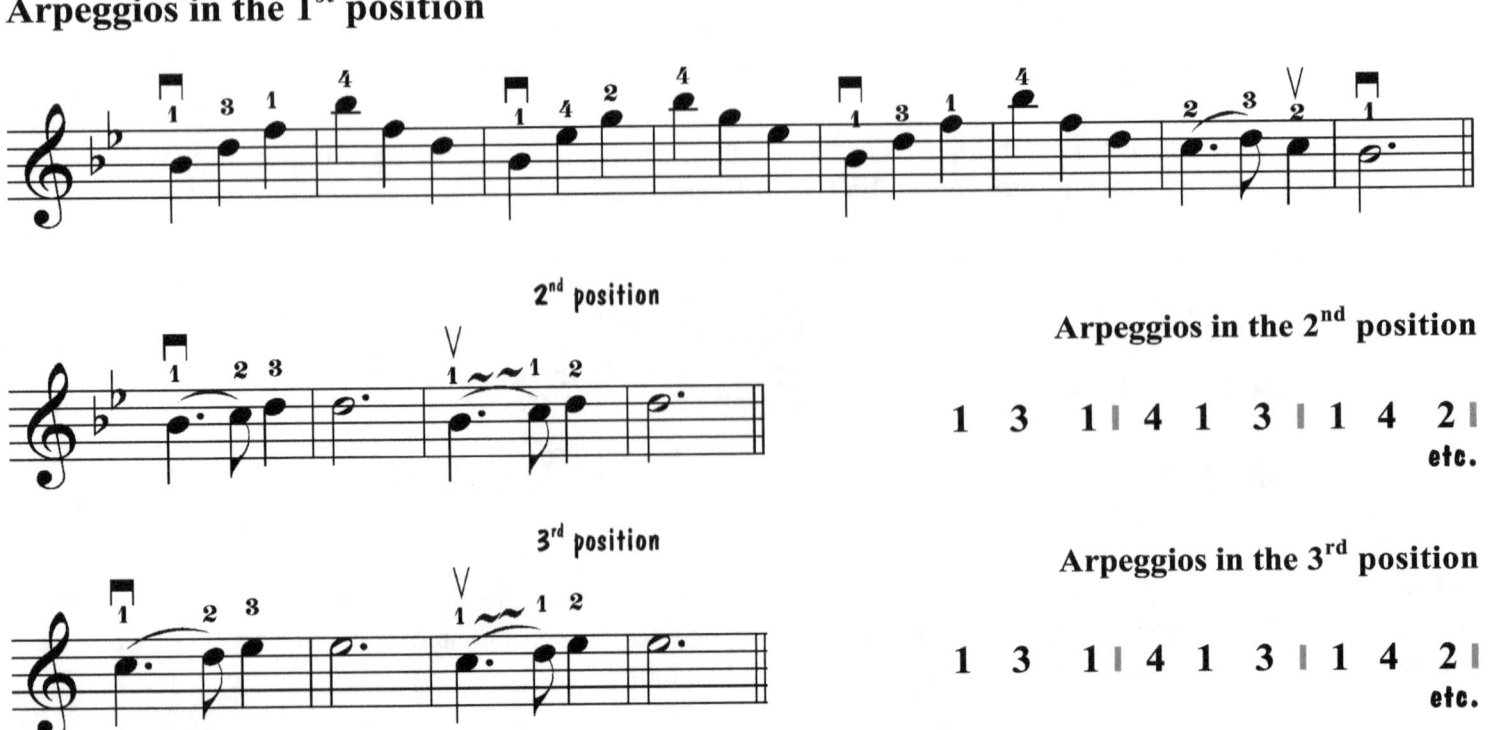

Arpeggios in the 2nd position

1   3   1 | 4   1   3 | 1   4   2 |
                                  etc.

Arpeggios in the 3rd position

1   3   1 | 4   1   3 | 1   4   2 |
                                  etc.

What do you see here?

A violinist with nine fingers?

A centipede?

Three pictures in one?

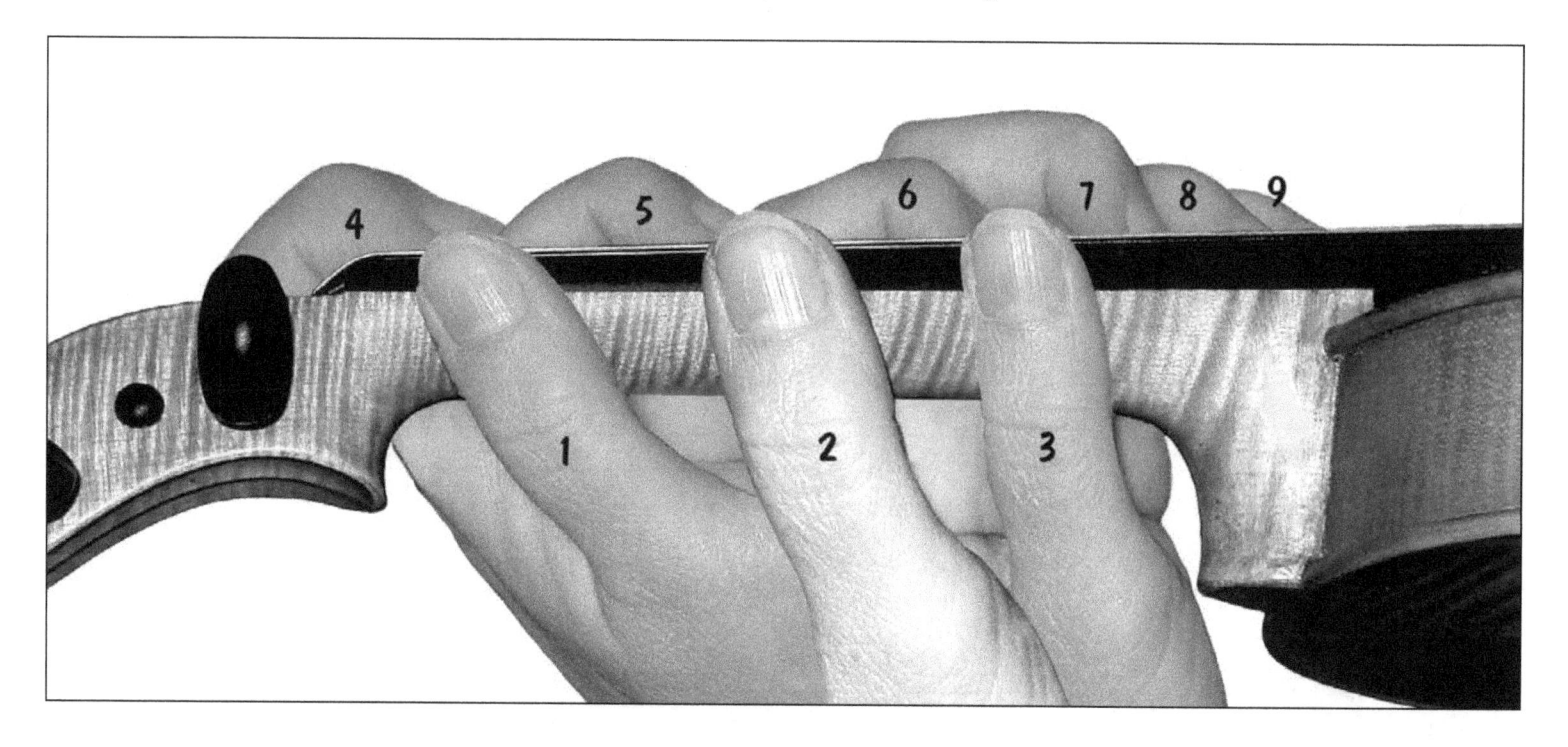

That's right! Here are three photographs combined into one.
Examine this composite photograph carefully and answer the following questions.
The rule concerning left hand posture at the bottom of the page will help!

1a. In which position is thumb number 1? _____
1b. Which numbered finger is directly across from the thumb in this position? _____

2a. In which position is thumb number 2? _____
2b. Which numbered finger is directly across from the thumb in this position? _____

3a. In which position is thumb number 3? _____
3b. Which numbered finger is directly across from the thumb in this position? _____

4. In which position are fingers 7, 8 and 9 playing? _____

Rule for Left Hand Posture in the 1st, 2nd and 3rd Positions

The thumb is always directly across from the first finger.
Its location clearly indicates the position in which a violinist is playing.

Trill Exercise in the 1st, 2nd and 3rd Positions

Here you will practice many things in a short time:
Playing *forte* at the tip; listening for resonance; improving intonation;
a confident feel for the individual positions; and many upper mordents and trills.

Preparatory Exercise

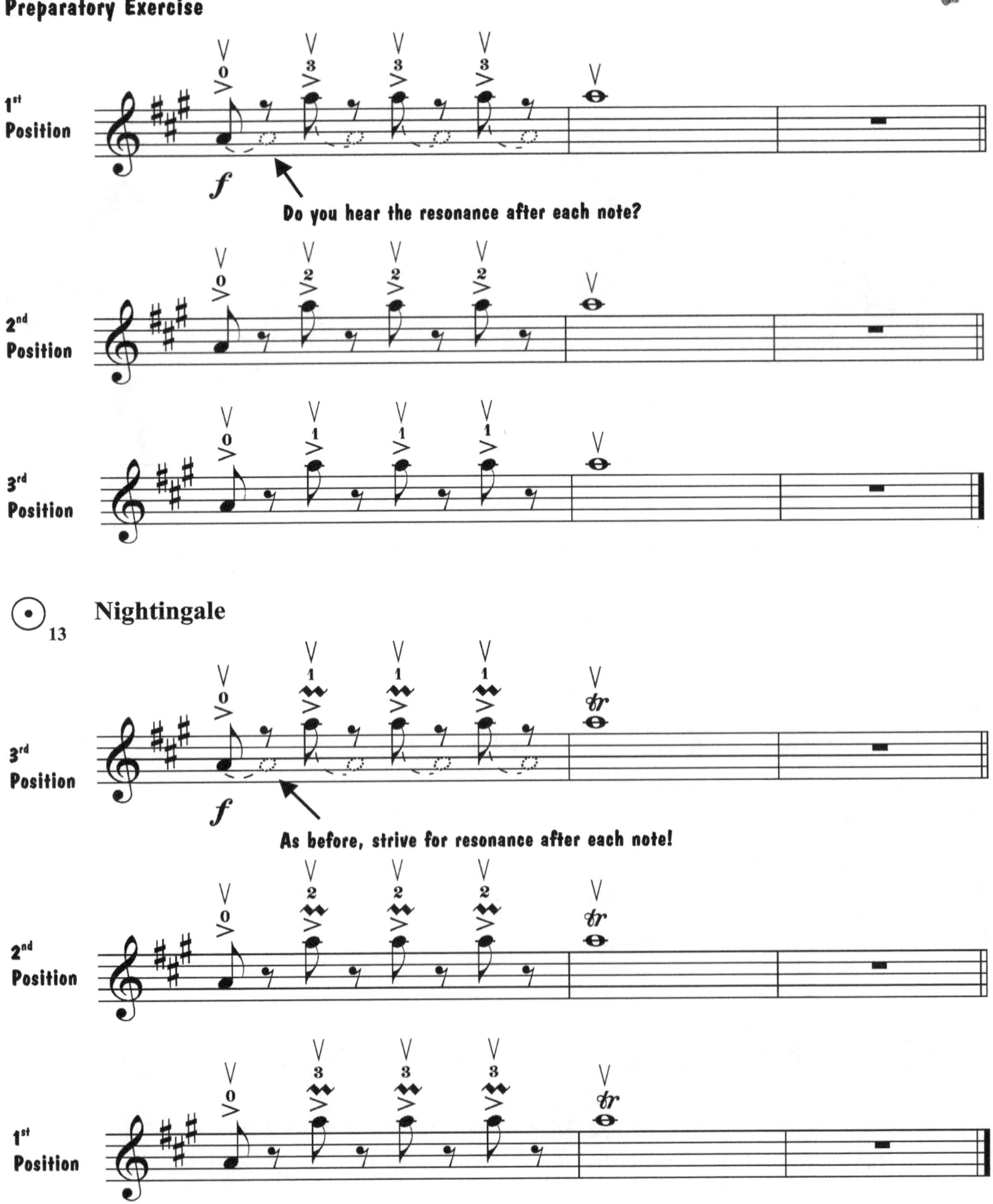

1st Position

f
Do you hear the resonance after each note?

2nd Position

3rd Position

⊙ 13 **Nightingale**

3rd Position

f
As before, strive for resonance after each note!

2nd Position

1st Position

Exercise with Fourths

Preparation (changing from an open string to the 4th finger)

STOP! Arm guidance
STOP! Arm guidance
STOP! Arm guidance

14 Second Fall Melody (with the 1st and 4th fingers)

Repeat the *First Fall Melody* in book 3A (p. 9) as well.

Chromatic Exercise

Snake Scale *(faster)*

Do you remember the Snake Scale from book 3A? Now you will play it significantly faster. First, play the exercise silently without the bow as you sing the snake scale. Strive for fluid, snake-like sliding movements of your fingers without changing your wrist or thumb postures.

Bow Exercises

You are already familiar with these sketches from the earlier books. They should remind you of some important points:

Silent String Crossings

There should be no sound between the notes.

Compact String Crossings

The string crossing movement should be as small as possible.

Resonant Double Stops

Bow both strings simultaneously and don't use any more weight than you would during tuning.

Bow exercises across two strings

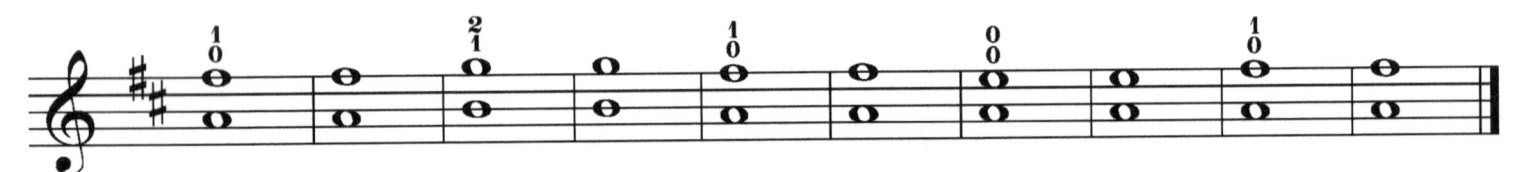

Play this exercise with the following bowings:

Three practice suggestions:

- **From slow to fast bow strokes:** Begin by practicing all of the bowing variations very slowly. Strive towards small, compact string crossing movements and a resonant tone. When you can play a variation beautifully, gradually increase the tempo.
- **From short to broad bow strokes:** Begin by playing all notes short and perform the string crossings during the rests between notes. When you can do this well, begin using more bow for each repetition.
- **From the A/E strings to the D/A and G/D strings:** Perform these exercises on the two lower string pairs as well.

Invent some bowings of your own:

Bow exercises across three strings

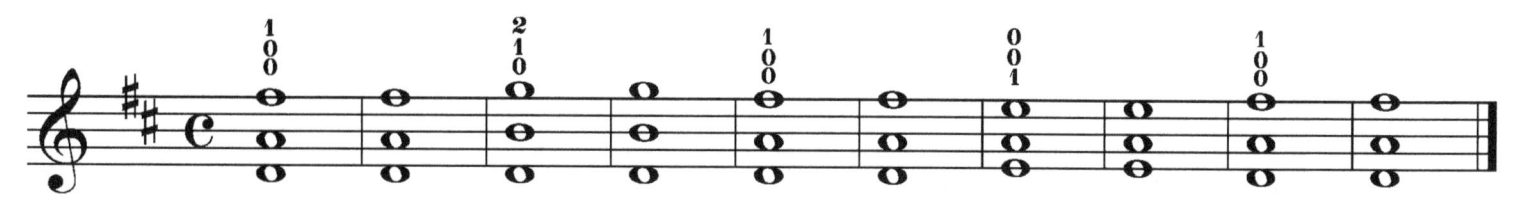

Bowings:

Play these exercises on the lower strings as well; G, D and A strings!

Invent some bowings of your own:

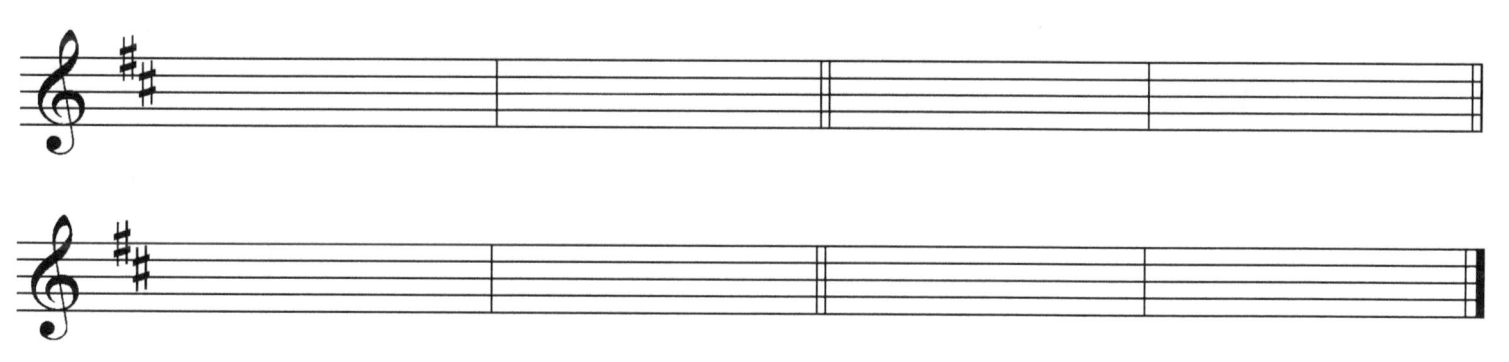

The String Crossing Orchestra

All of the preceding exercises can be performed simultaneously. Try this in a group lesson. Begin by playing only two of the bowing variations, then gradually add more and more voices. A total of 14 variations are written out on these two pages. By adding your own variations, the group might pluck and bow over 20 different parts. It is crucial that everyone plays very rhythmically so that you stay together. Adding a piano accompaniment will be very helpful!

Gavotte

Jean Becker

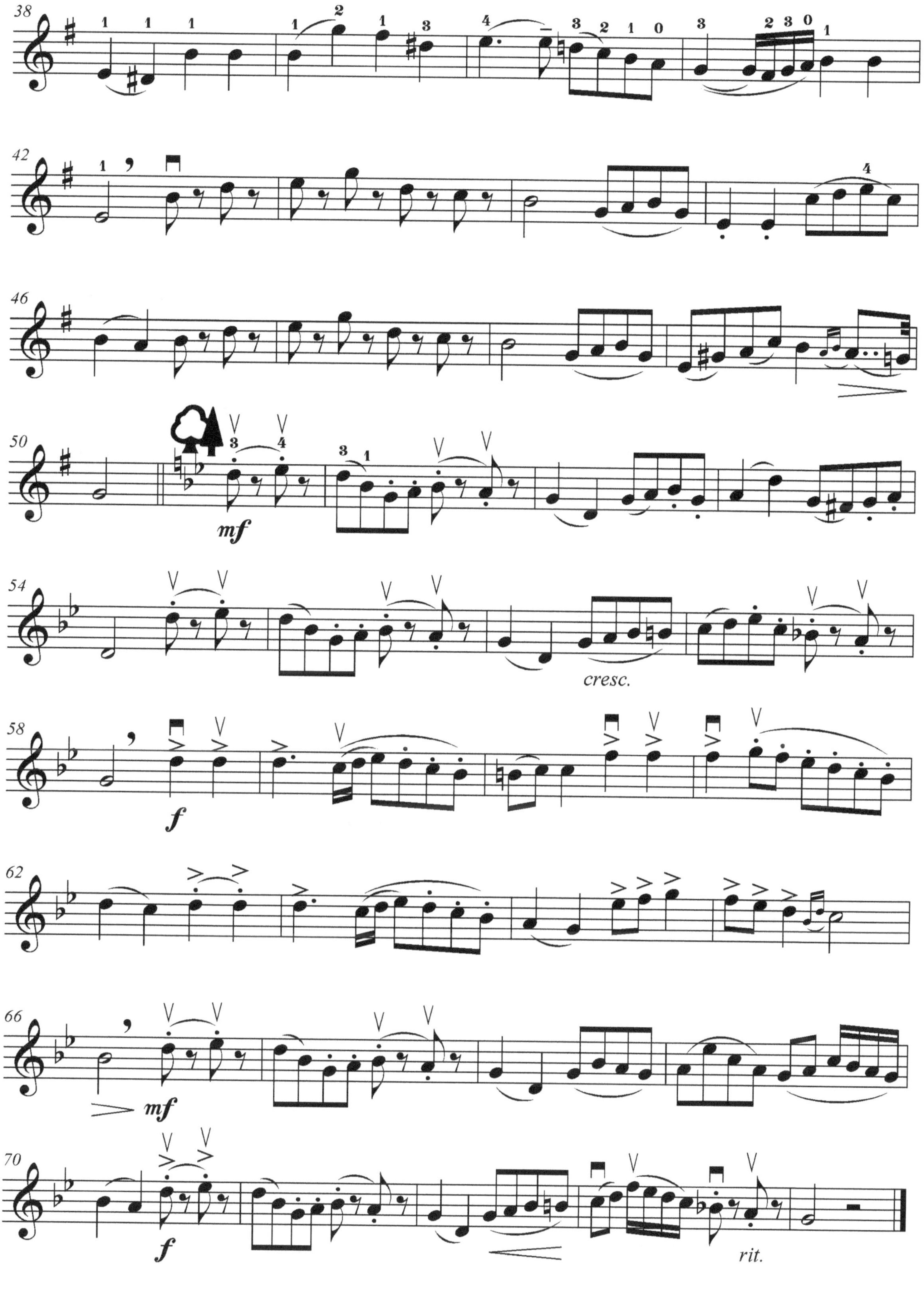
38
42
46
50
mf
54
cresc.
58
f
62
66
mf
70
f
rit.

Your new piece – Gavotte by Becker

As you listen to your new piece, pay special attention to its three-part (*ternary*) form.

| A1 | B | A2 | C | D | C | A1 | B | A2 |

The beginning ...

... with the four different endings

ending 1

ending 2

ending 3

ending 4

At first, practice the 3rd and 4th endings very slowly with portato bowing!

The B-flat major scale

Listen very carefully, making sure that the eighth notes at the frog and at the tip sound the same. Try beginning this scale with an up bow as well.

w.b.   tip   w.b.   frog

Begin each up bow with a crackle, like a mouse biting into a nut six times with its small teeth: **BITE, BITE, BITE, BITE, BITE, BITE.**

w.b.   w.b.

Part B in four small exercises

1st Exercise: Play the three notes with lots of energy and bow.

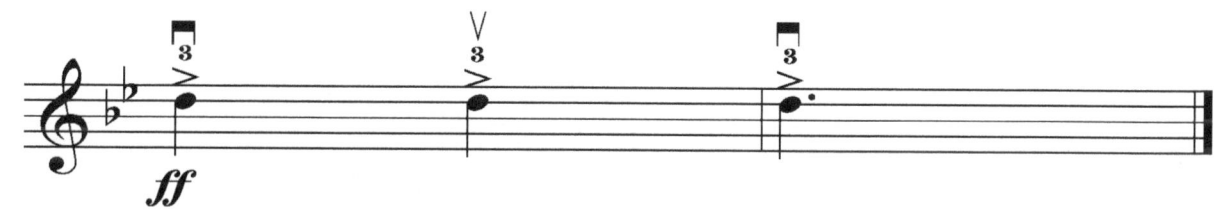

ff

2nd Exercise: Play the following three notes at the tip with very little bow.

3rd Exercise: Add three small up bows to the notes from the 1st and 2nd exercises.

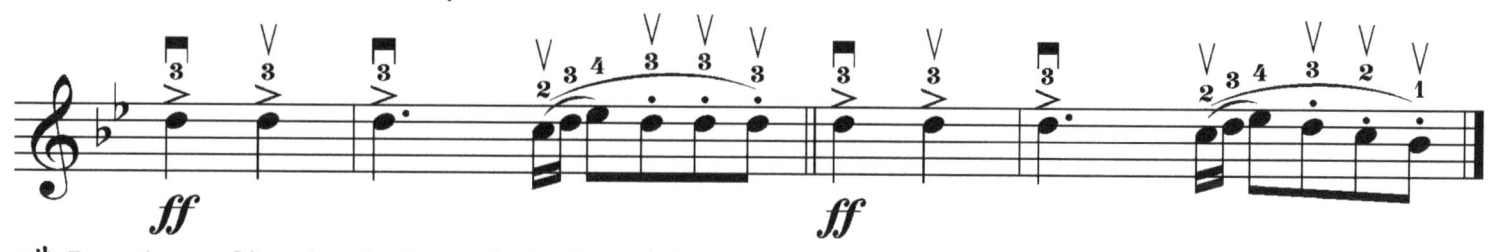

ff   *ff*

4th Exercise: Play the rhythm with the low 1st finger, then slide it to its high position. Make sure that your finger has accurately arrived at its new position before you begin bowing the next rhythm.

STOP!   STOP!

The entire subsection B

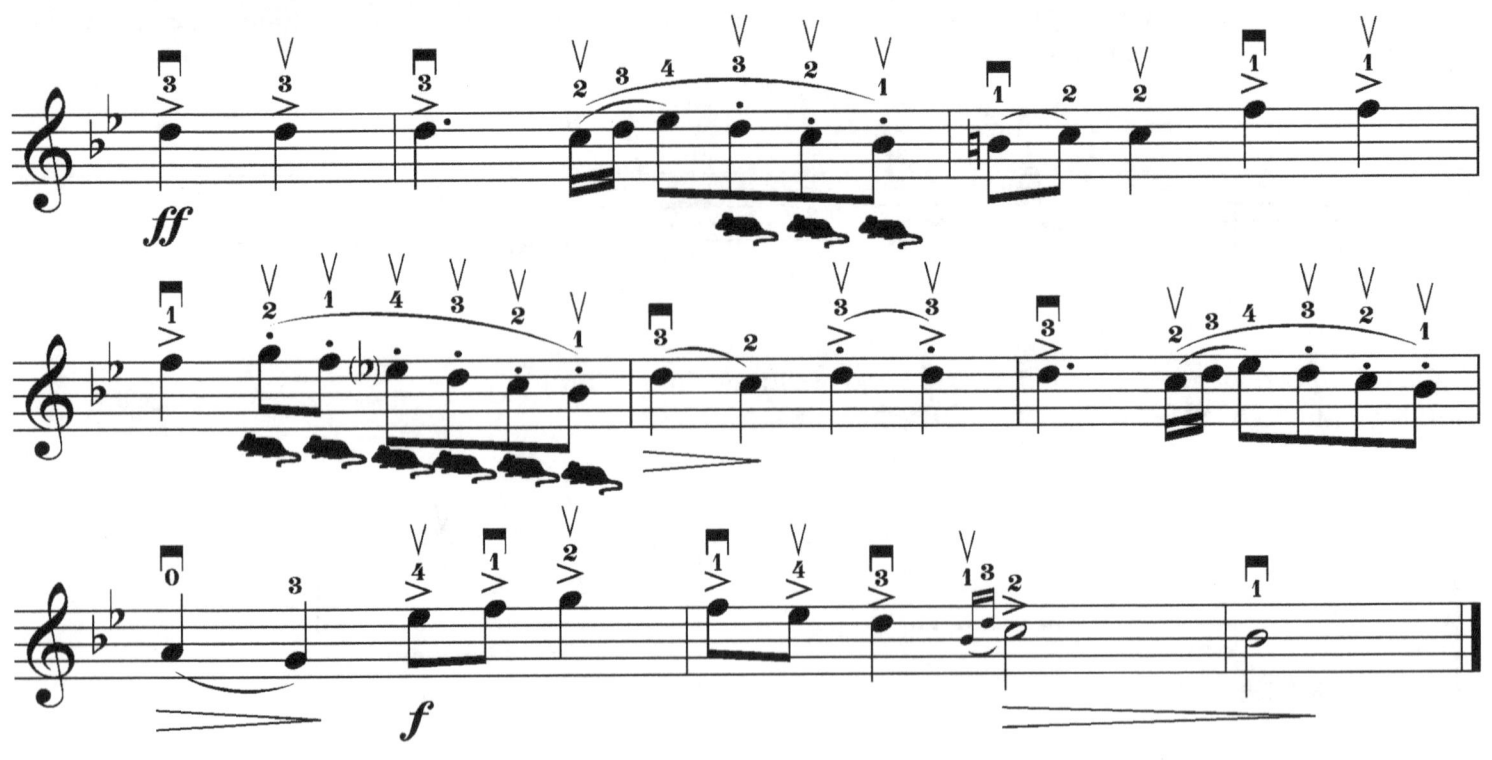

The difficult measures in subsection C made easy!

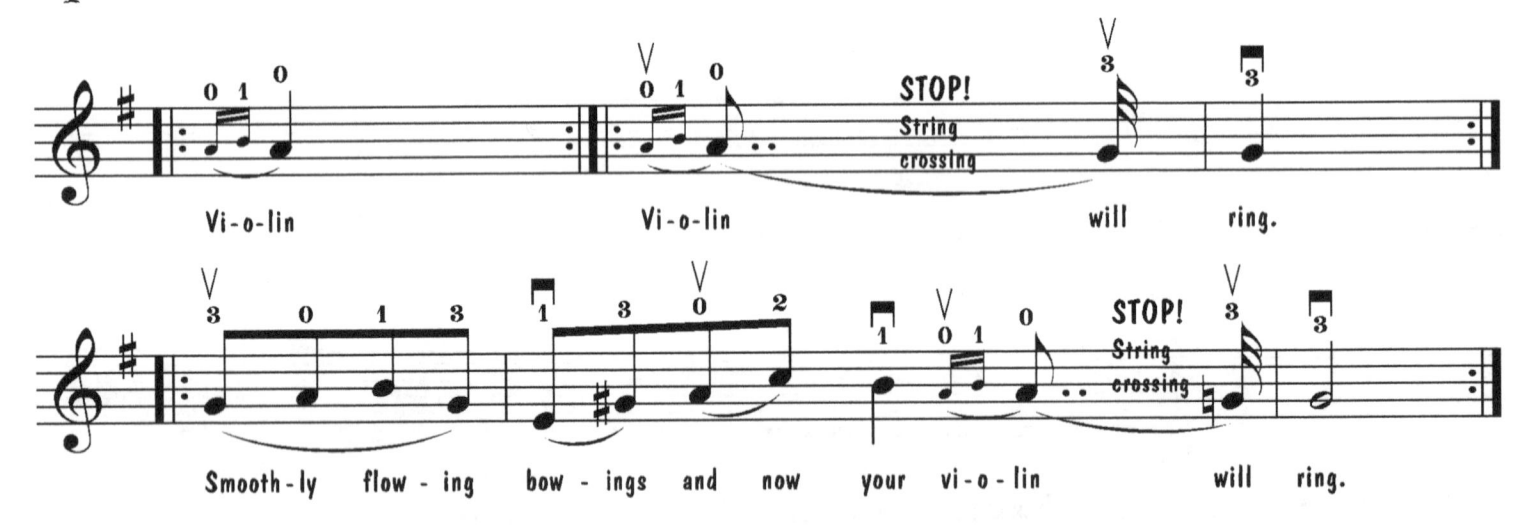

Vi-o-lin   Vi-o-lin   STOP! String crossing   will ring.

Smooth-ly flow-ing bow-ings and now your vi-o-lin   STOP! String crossing   will ring.

The change from vigorous to gentler, flowing bow strokes

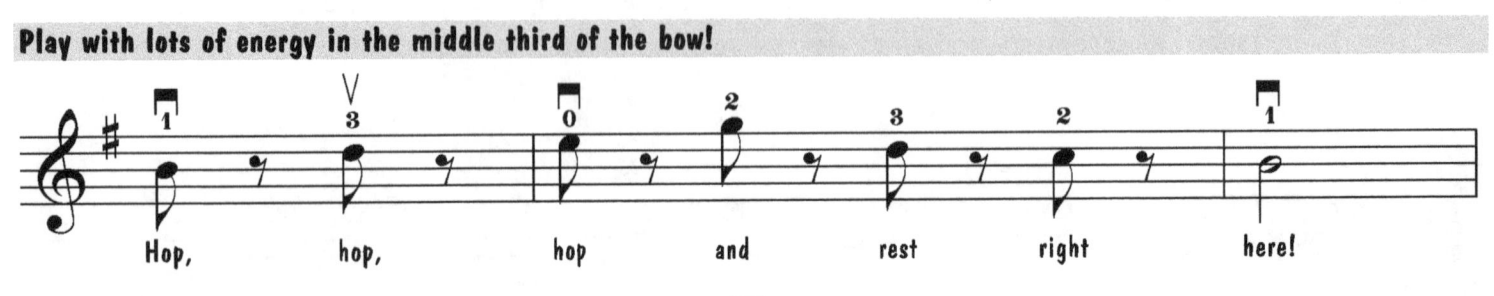

Play with lots of energy in the middle third of the bow!

Hop,   hop,   hop   and   rest   right   here!

Continue with gentle flowing strokes!

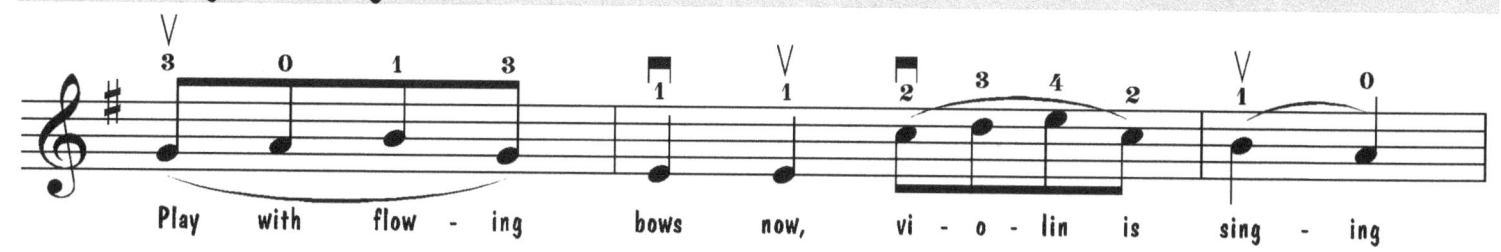

Play with flow-ing bows now, vi-o-lin is sing-ing

Play again with lots of energy in the middle third of the bow!

Hop, hop, hop and rest once more!

Change again to gentle flowing strokes!

Smooth-ly flow-ing bow-ings and now your vi-o-lin will ring.

STOP! String crossing

Subsection D:
Energetic, powerful strokes with lots of bow

f

Now you have learned all sections of the Gavotte and can begin putting them together in context.

16-19
16. Gavotte 🍀 A1 — in a slow practice tempo
17. Gavotte 🍀 B — in a slow practice tempo
18. Gavotte 🍀 A2 — in a slow practice tempo
19. Gavotte ✺ C to the end — in a slow practice tempo

20-22
20. Gavotte 🍀 — in performance tempo
21. Gavotte ✺ — in performance tempo
22. Gavotte 🍀 — in performance tempo

Double Stop Exercises and Songs

Short but sweet - very important double stop exercises

Listen To Me - double stops with the melody in the upper voice

Lis - ten to me, how my vi - o - lin is sing - ing.
Two strings at once, this is real - ly lots of fun.
Lis - ten to me, how my vi - o - lin is ring - ing.

Lullaby - double stops with the melody in the upper voice

Sleep my child, close your eyes. All the stars are shin - ing.
And the moon, he's com-ing soon, see his face is smil - ing. Rock my
cra - dle, go to sleep. Close your eyes, now, fall a - sleep.

Come and Watch My Little Kitty - double stops with the melody in the lower voice

Preparatory exercise: While playing only the open E string, finger the lower notes!

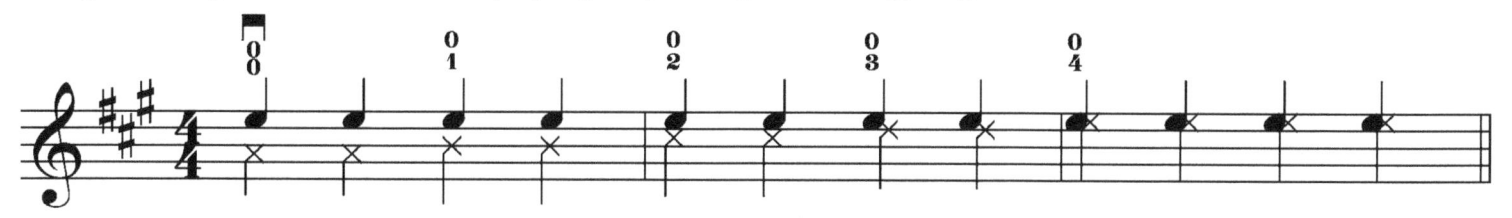

Song

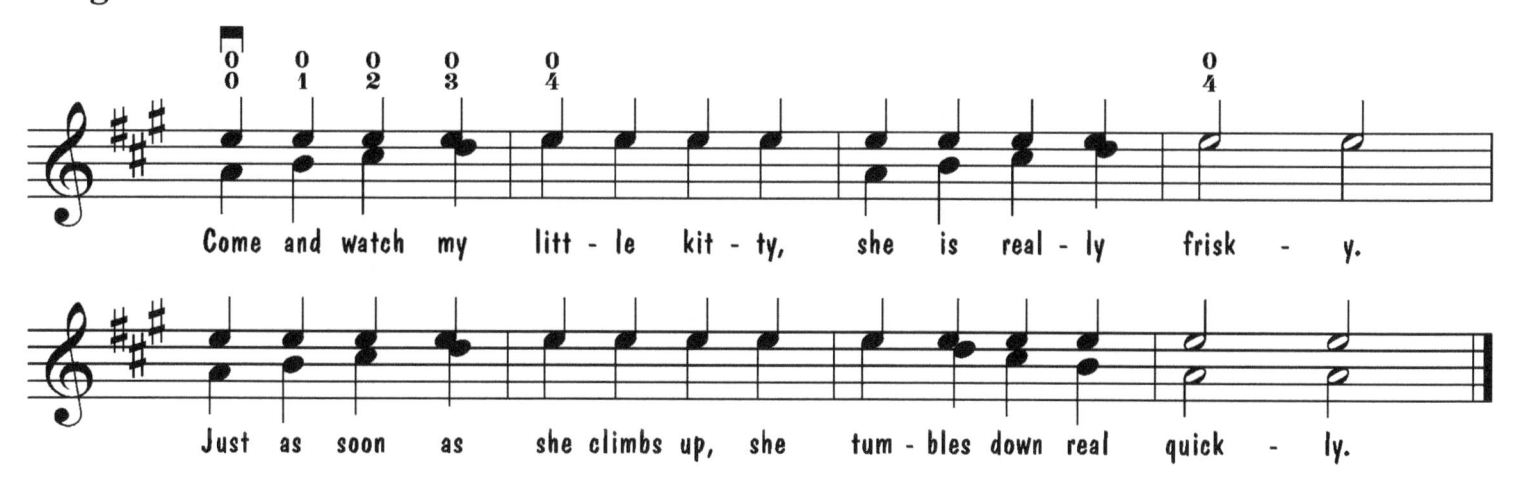

Come and watch my litt-le kit-ty, she is real-ly frisk-y.
Just as soon as she climbs up, she tum-bles down real quick-ly.

Lightly Row - double stops with the melody in the lower voice

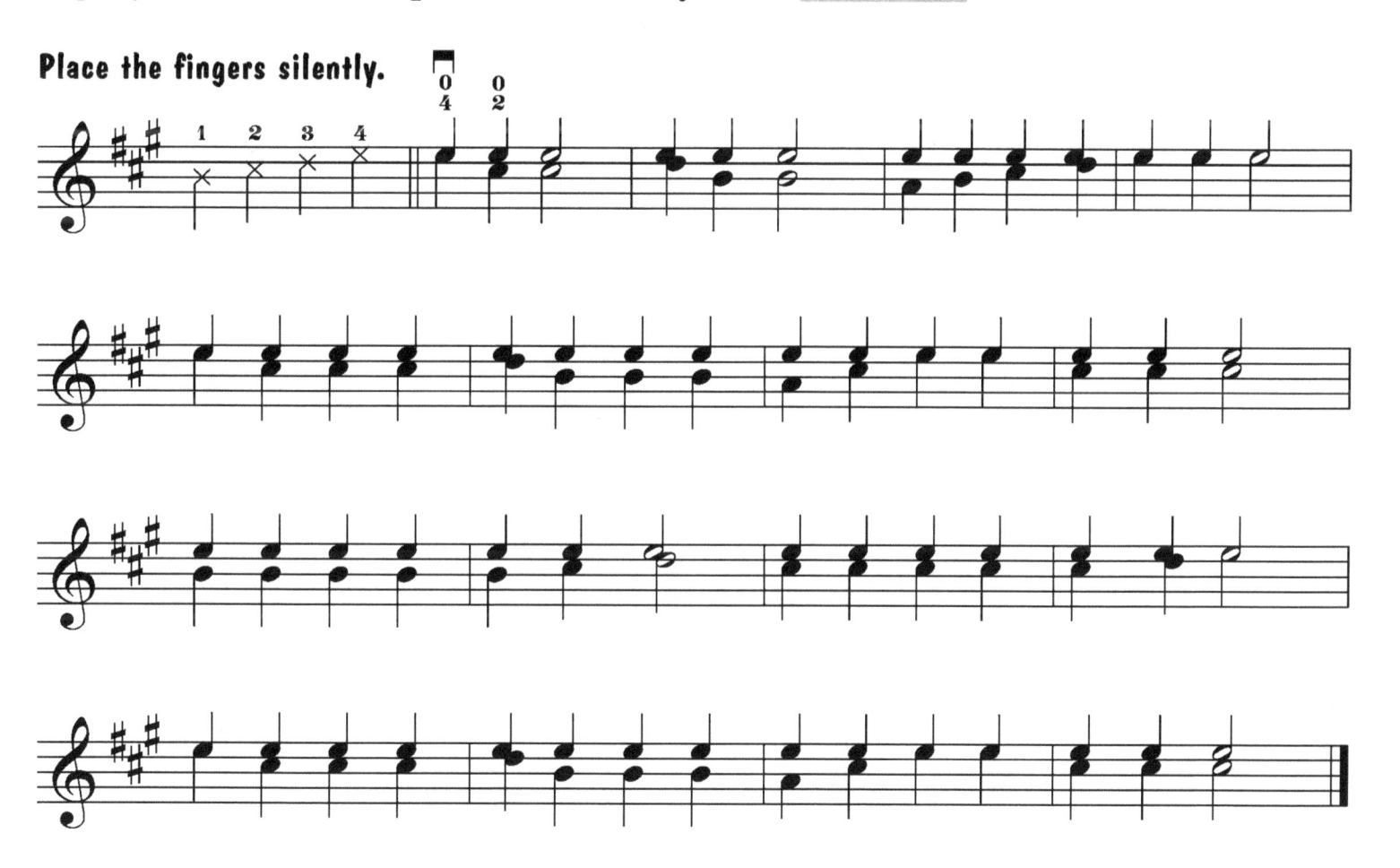

Place the fingers silently.

23. Hej! Haj! - Hungarian Dance

Play all eighth notes lively and short!
Begin slowly and gradually increase the tempo!

Double Stops Are So Much Fun

Preparatory Exercises

- **Double stops with one fingered note** and an accompanying open string in the upper or lower voice
- **Double stops with two fingered notes**
- **Three-note chords**

Try the following: Finger both notes of each double stop but only bow the melody note.

Dou - ble stops are so much fun. Keep them rin - ging one by one.

Double Stops Are So Much Fun

Dou - ble stops are so much fun. Keep them rin - ging one by one.

mf

Dou - ble stops are so much fun. Keep them rin - ging one by one.

f

27

Gavotte I and II

**From the Orchestral Suite No. 3 in D Major, BWV 1068
in a transcription for violin and piano**

Johann Sebastian Bach

Gavotte I

Gavotte II

🔘 25 Your new piece – Gavotte I and II by Johann Sebastian Bach

These two movements come from the Orchestral Suite No. 3 in D Major, BWV 1068. Maybe your parents have a CD with an original orchestral version of this piece. If not, your teacher will certainly be able to play a CD with this orchestral work for you.

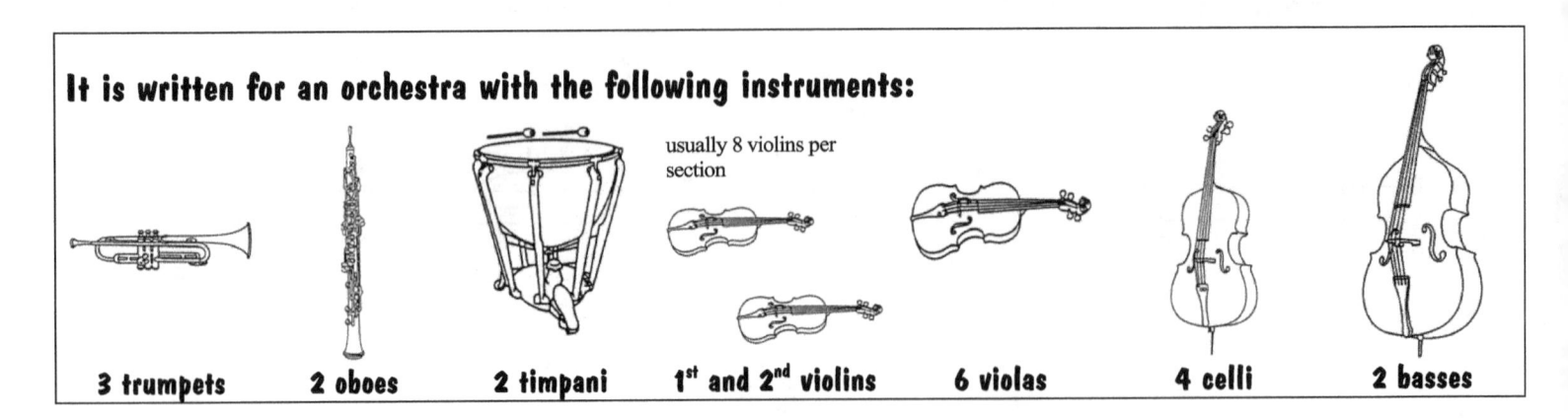

It is written for an orchestra with the following instruments:

3 trumpets | 2 oboes | 2 timpani | 1st and 2nd violins (usually 8 violins per section) | 6 violas | 4 celli | 2 basses

The brilliant sound of the trumpets combined with the booming of the timpani give this piece a particularly festive character. Try to play Gavotte I and II along with the orchestral version. You will certainly enjoy being accompanied by such a majestic sound.

This is what the beginning of the score looks like:

What exactly is a score?

A score is typically a very thick music book in which all parts of a piece are written one below the other. It enables the conductor to see at a glance what each instrument in the orchestra is playing.

Gavotte I

[Score excerpt with parts for trumpet 1, trumpet 2, trumpet 3, timpani, oboe 1, oboe 2, violin 1, violin 2, viola, cello and contrabass]

30

Listening exercises for the orchestral version

1. Can you hear the individual instruments?
2. Look at the score. When the piece begins, all instruments are playing. Which instruments do you hear the most?
3. After a few measures, which four instruments have rests?
4. Listen to the first section of Gavotte I. Which instruments play louder? The trumpets and timpani with the strings, or the oboes with the strings?
5. Study your violin part on page 28. Which dynamics appear in the first section (up to the first repeat sign)? Which instruments play during *forte* and which play during *mezzoforte*?

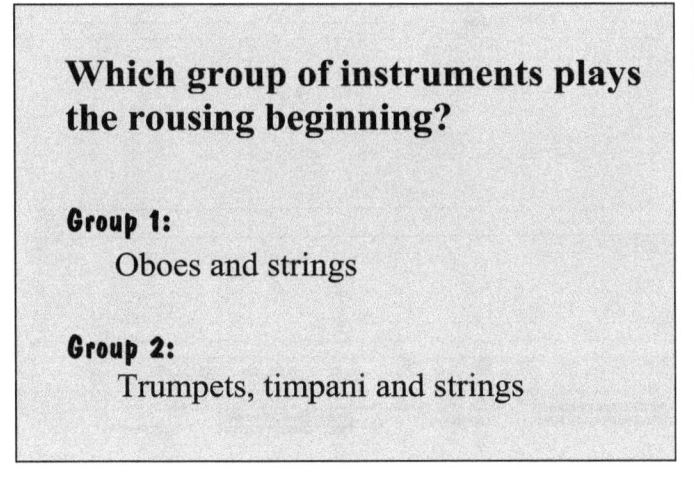

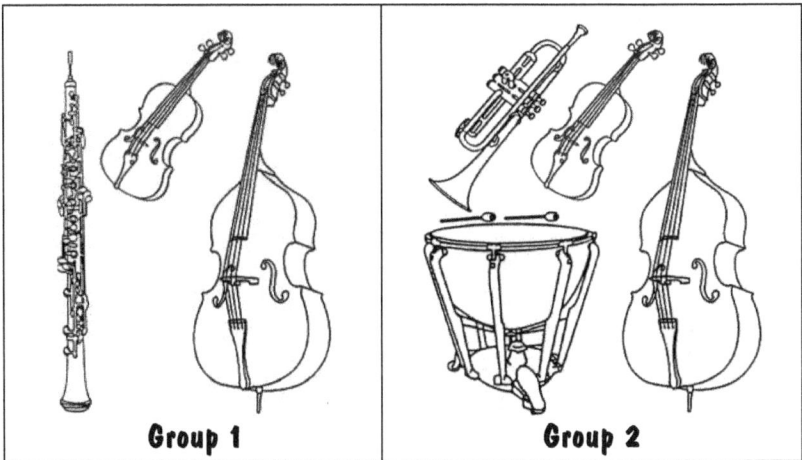

Which group of instruments plays the rousing beginning?

Group 1:
   Oboes and strings

Group 2:
   Trumpets, timpani and strings

The beginning measures of Gavotte I

Play the beginning notes, paying special attention to a good bow distribution. Can you imagine the sound of the orchestra?

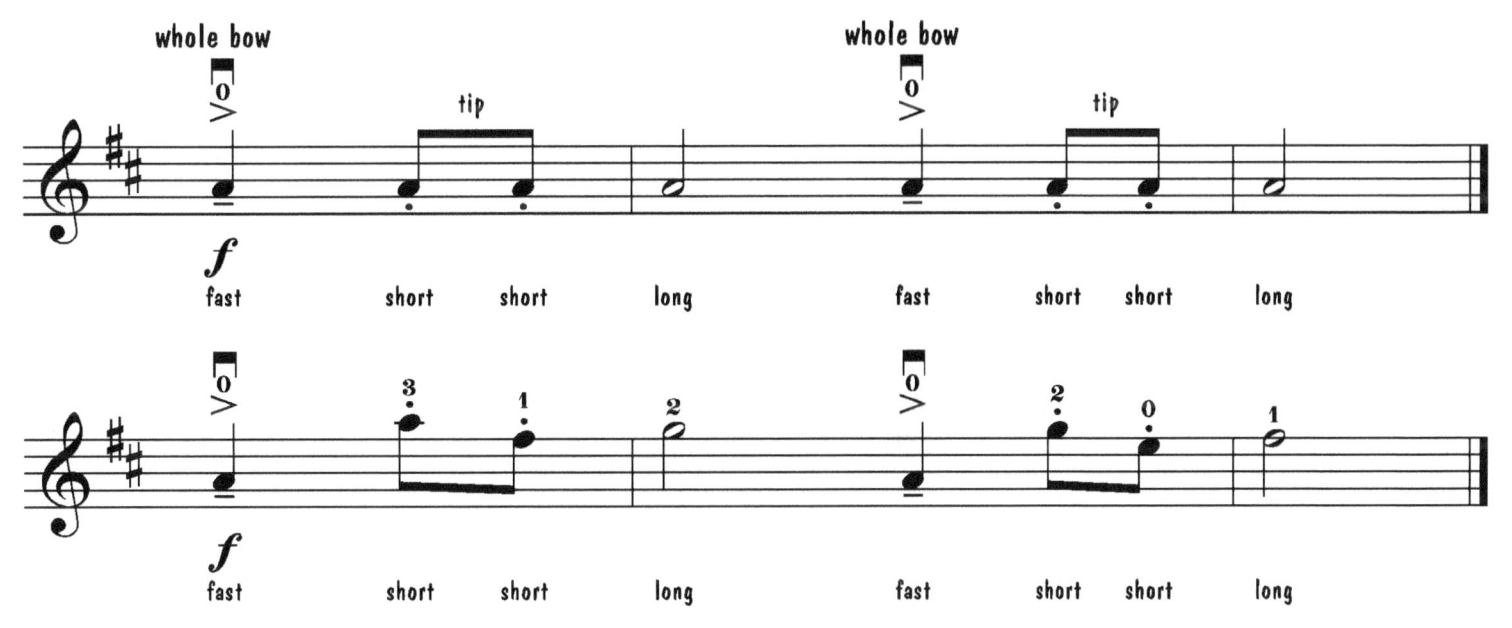

What exactly does the abbreviation "BWV" mean?

This is the abbreviation for

*Bach-Werke-Verzeichnis (Bach-Works-Catalogue),
the thematic catalog of the works of J. S. Bach.*

All of Bach's compositions are listed and numbered using the abbreviation *BWV*.

The appoggiaturas in measures 1 and 2

Stress the second note of the slur. For clarity, say the word „*hel*-**lo**" as you play the slur (with the accent on the second syllable). In the second section of Gavotte I, this emphasis will be turned around in four places. There, you should stress the first note of the slur.

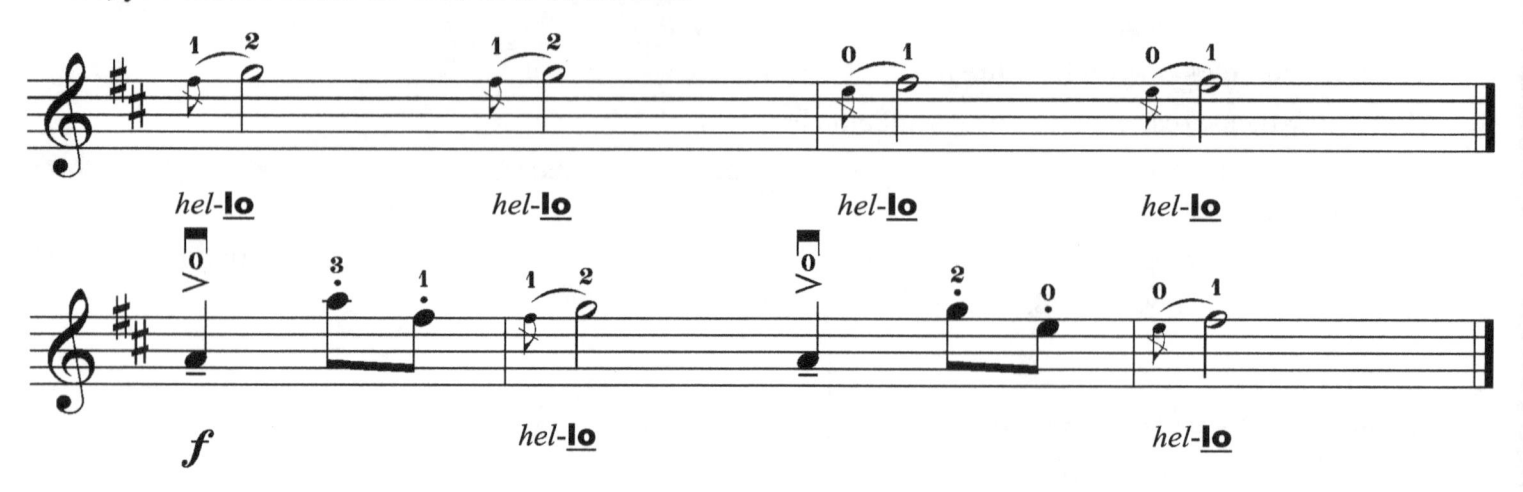

hel-**lo**   hel-**lo**   hel-**lo**   hel-**lo**

f   hel-**lo**   hel-**lo**

The two passages with the low and high first fingers

hel-*lo*

26. Gavotte I, 1ˢᵗ section - in a slow practice tempo
27. Gavotte I, 2ⁿᵈ section - in a slow practice tempo
(26-27)

Clarification of the Appoggiaturas

There are numerous books with long, theoretical explanations of how appoggiaturas should be played. An appoggiatura's execution depends on several factors: the musical period, the musical genre, the composer, and sometimes even the performer.

In this phase, we want to perform the appoggiaturas as follows:

Appoggiatura BEFORE the beat	**Appoggiatura ON the beat**
A small eighth note with a single stroke through the stem	A small eighth note WITHOUT the stem struck through
Hel-**lo** We stress the **main note**.	**Hel**-*lo* We stress the **appoggiatura note**.

Gavotte II

The bow scheme for the first phrase on the A string

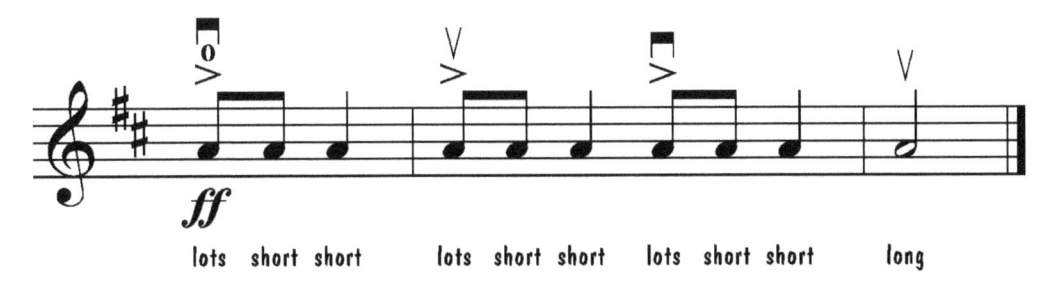

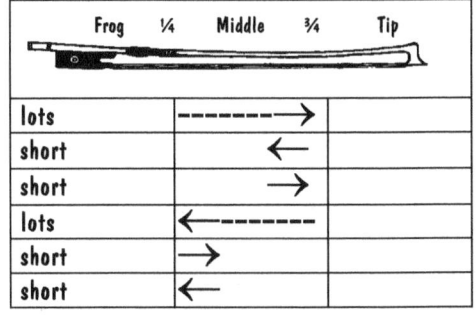

lots short short   lots short short   lots short short   long

The first phrase: Vigorous bow strokes

The second phrase: Small, delicate strokes at the balance point

The difficult eighth-note passage with the high third finger

STOP! Place high 3rd finger with 4th finger right next to it.

How old are you? Perhaps you are 8 years old?

Then you should play this exercise eight times in a row without mistakes.
In any case, this passage must be practiced both frequently and carefully.

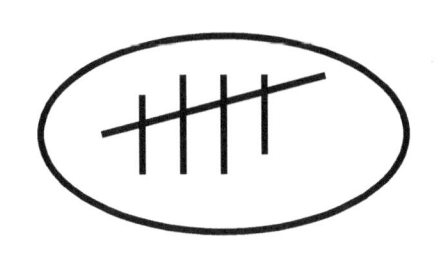

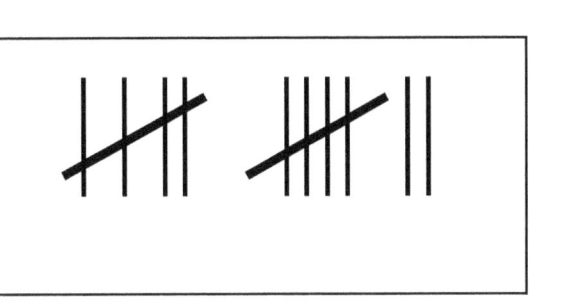

33

The silent cradle with seven different string levels

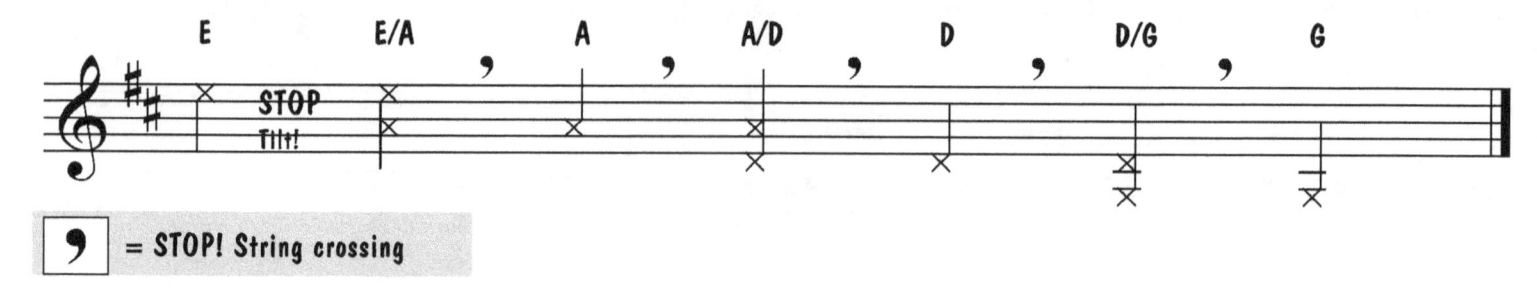

❩ = STOP! String crossing

Before beginning your bow stroke, set the bow on the string and practice this silent exercise. Try landing on the correct string(s) with your eyes closed.

The change from one to two voices in four small steps

1st Step: The melody on the E string

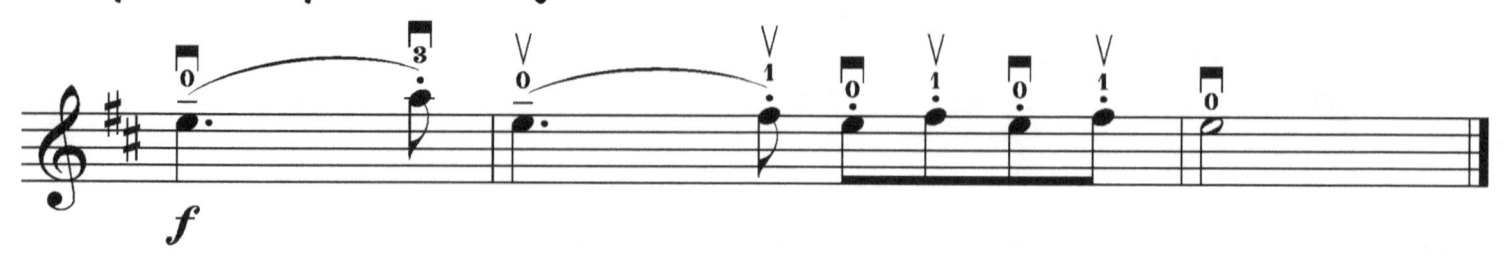

2nd Step: Three short double stop exercises

⎯⎯⎯ = keep finger down

3rd Step: The melody with an open A string accompaniment

4th Step: The passage as it appears in the piece

Preparatory exercise for the bow scheme in measures 26-27

> Begin the first down bow at the balance point and return to the balance point with each up bow.

> The same principle applies here: Begin the down bow at the balance point and return to this point with each up bow. Down and up bows should use the same amount of bow.

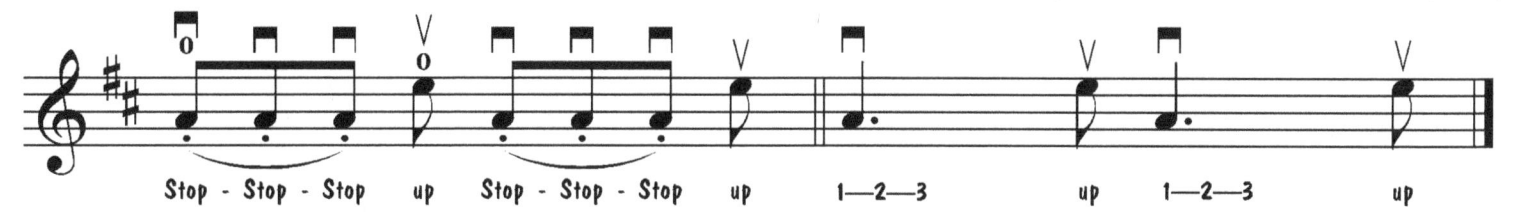

Stop - Stop - Stop   up   Stop - Stop - Stop   up   1—2—3   up   1—2—3   up

Measures 26-27, first with portato bowing and then with the slurs

Try to play the entire passage in the middle third of the bow.

Stop - Stop - Stop   up   Stop - Stop - Stop   up   Stop - Stop - Stop   up   slur - rrr   ti   ti   push   push

slur - rrr - rrr   up   slur - rrr - rrr   up   slur - rrr - rrr   up   slur - rrr   ti   ti   push   push

⊙ 28-29
28. Gavotte II, 1st section - in a slow practice tempo
29. Gavotte II, 2nd section - in a slow practice tempo

Now you have learned all sections of the piece and can begin playing them together in context.

⊙ 30-31
30. Gavotte I - in a medium practice tempo
31. Gavotte II and da capo - in a medium practice tempo

⊙ 32-33
32. Gavotte I - in performance tempo
33. Gavotte II and da capo - in performance tempo

Paganini Motion

Kerstin Wartberg

🔘 34-42
34.-36. Paganini Motion - in a medium practice tempo
37.-39. Paganini Motion - in performance tempo
40.-42. Paganini Motion - in performance tempo (piano accompaniment)

1. "Butterfly Motion" (upwards)

simile (= similarly - perform in same style as previous measures)

2. Sixteen Staccato Notes in One Up Bow

Start at the tip. Now be careful to save bow!

3. Tiny Bow Strokes at the Balance Point

Use very little bow and play with active fingers. Can you also perform the string crossings for the grace notes with a relaxed and fluid finger motion?

4. Chords and Single Notes

5. String Crossings at the Tip, with Accents on the Melody Notes

Play with a light accent on each up bow, using your wrist for the string crossings.

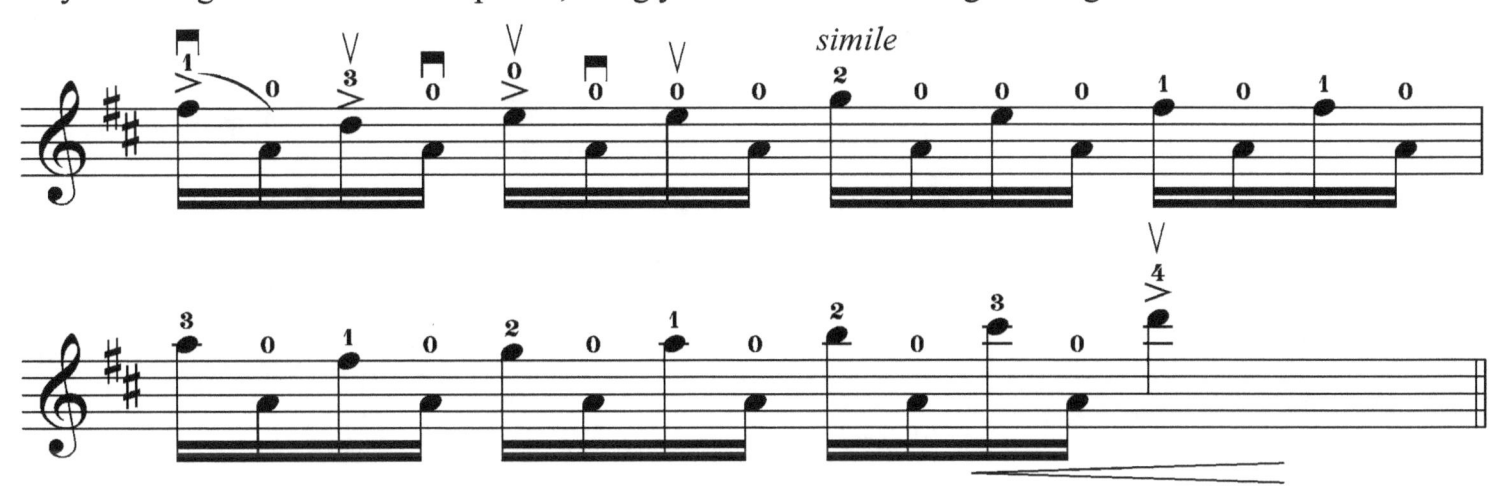

6. Triplets with Slurs and String Crossings

Play slightly below the middle of the bow, using your wrist and fingers. Use very little bow!

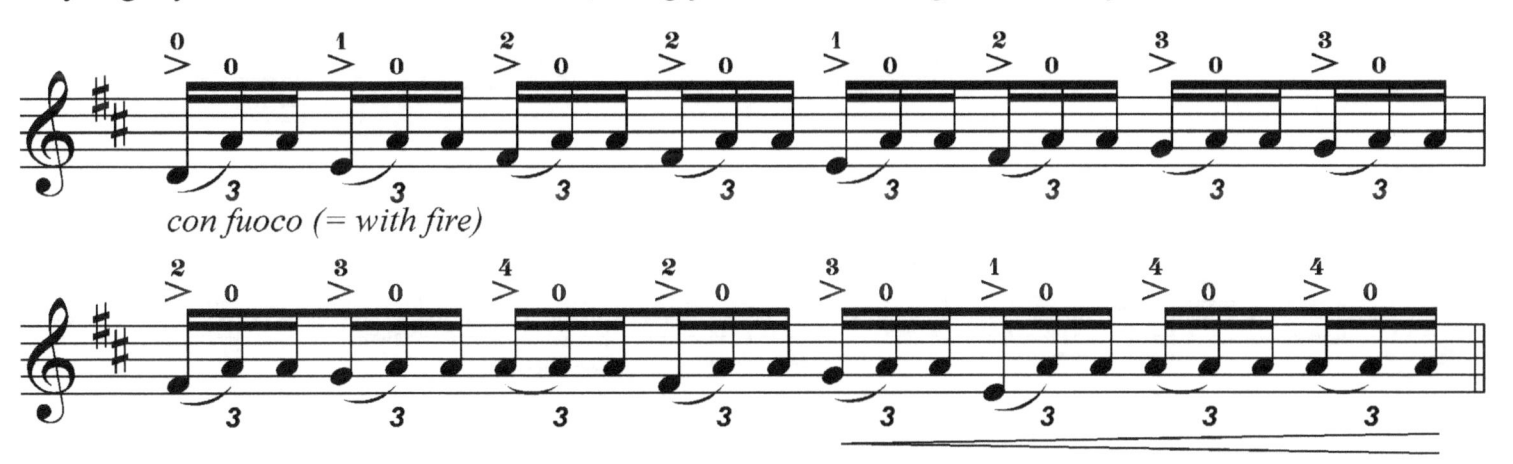

con fuoco (= with fire)

7. Fast Bowing with Double Stops

Here, too, play with very little bow and just below the middle.

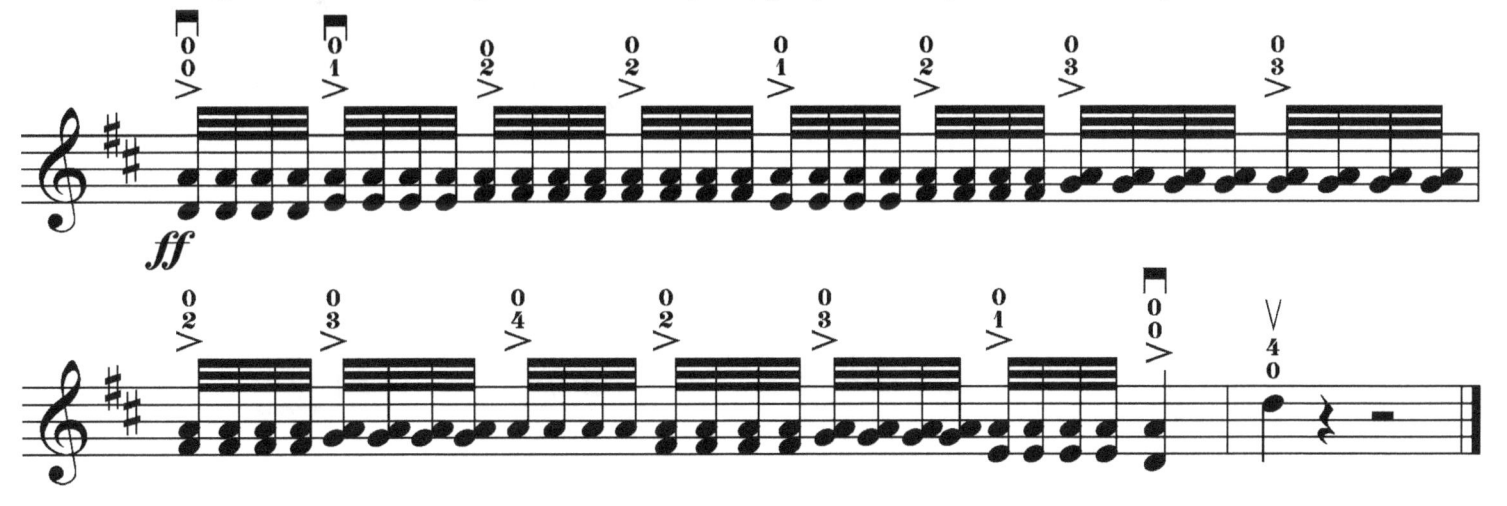

Bourrée

**From the Suite No. 3 for Violoncello Solo, BWV 1009
in a transcription for violin and piano**

Johann Sebastian Bach

Bourrée I

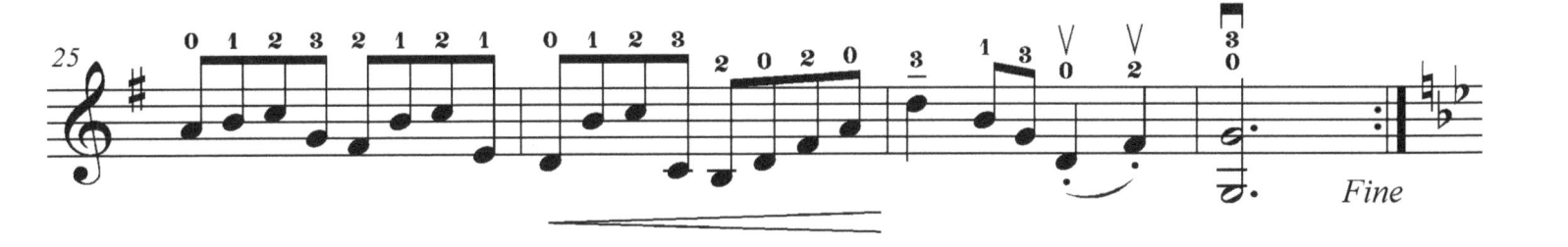

Bourrée II

Your new piece –
Bourrée by Johann Sebastian Bach

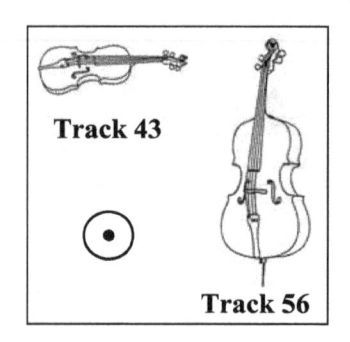

Listen to your new piece often.
You can choose either the transcription for violin and piano
or the original version for violoncello solo.

Track 43

Track 56

The beginning measures of *Bourrée*

Play energetically and let the music dance. The notes marked in gray should receive special emphasis and be played with an especially beautiful tone.

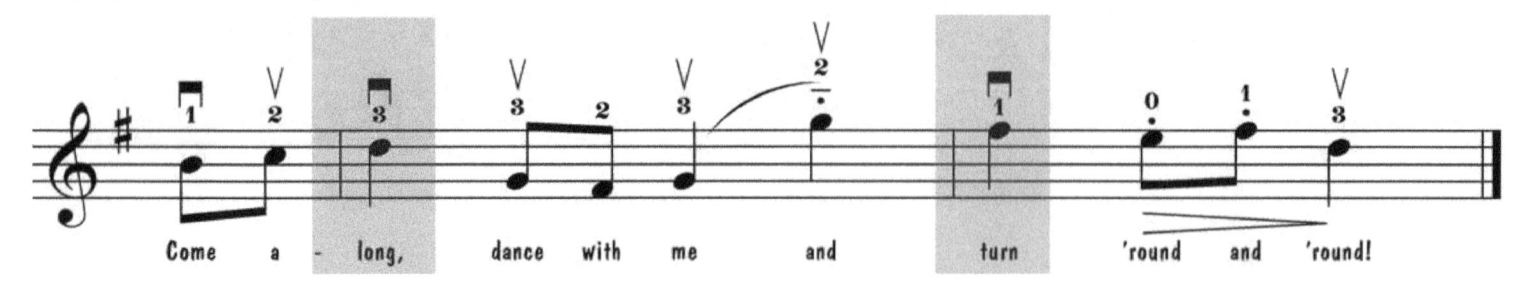

Come a - long, dance with me and turn 'round and 'round!

Preparatory exercises for the chord

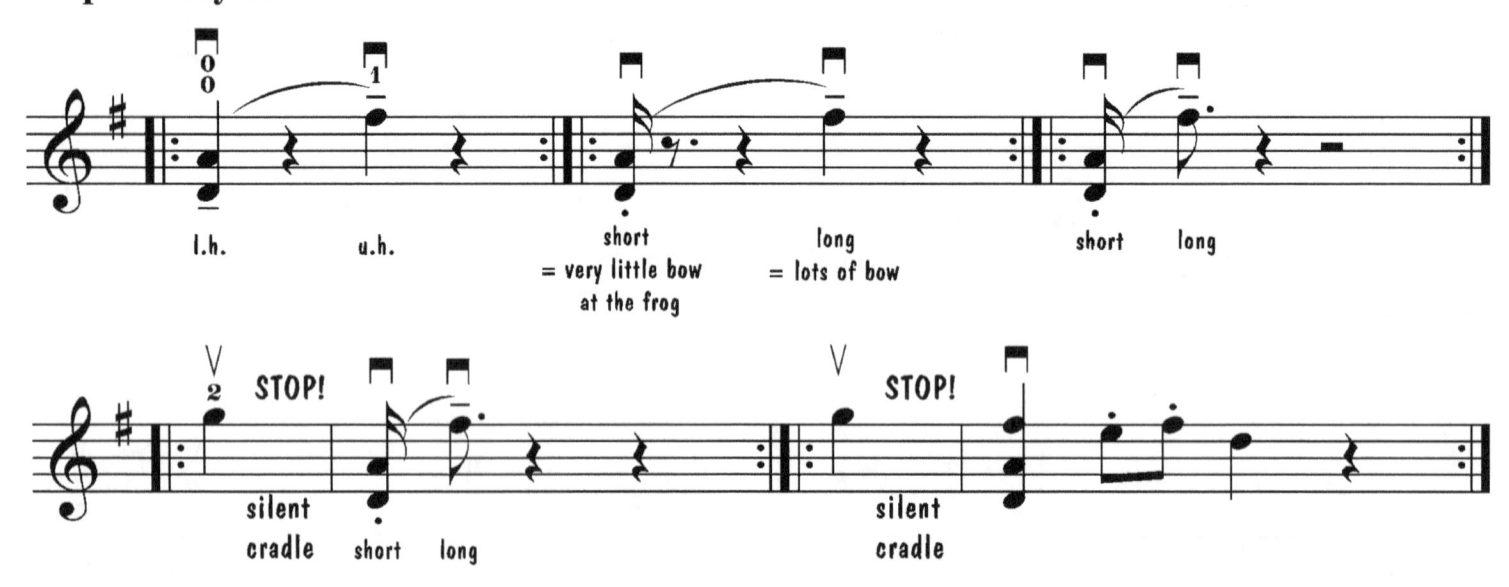

l.h.   u.h.   short   long   short   long
        = very little bow   = lots of bow
        at the frog

STOP!   STOP!
silent   silent
cradle short long   cradle

Trill exercise

Repeat the trill exercise on page 14 as well.

The beginning measures of *Bourrée* - embellished with a trill

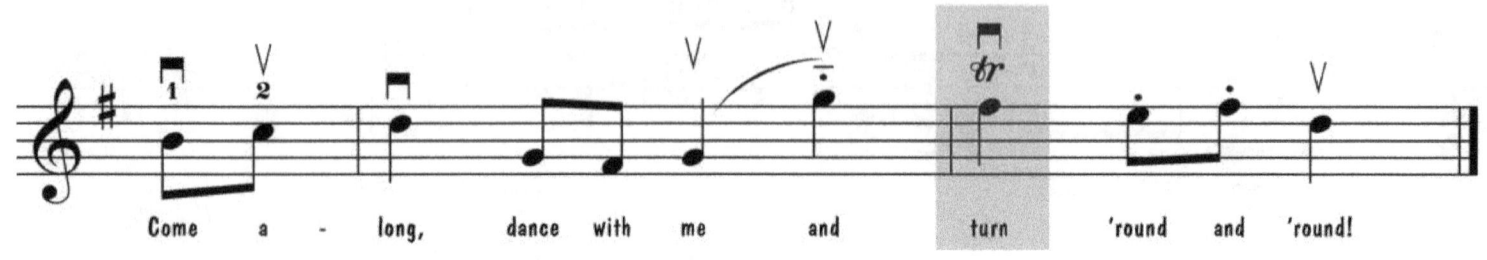

Come a - long, dance with me and turn 'round and 'round!

Preparatory exercises for the chord with the trill

**The string crossing passage (measures 5-6)
with STOP before all string crossings to a lower string**

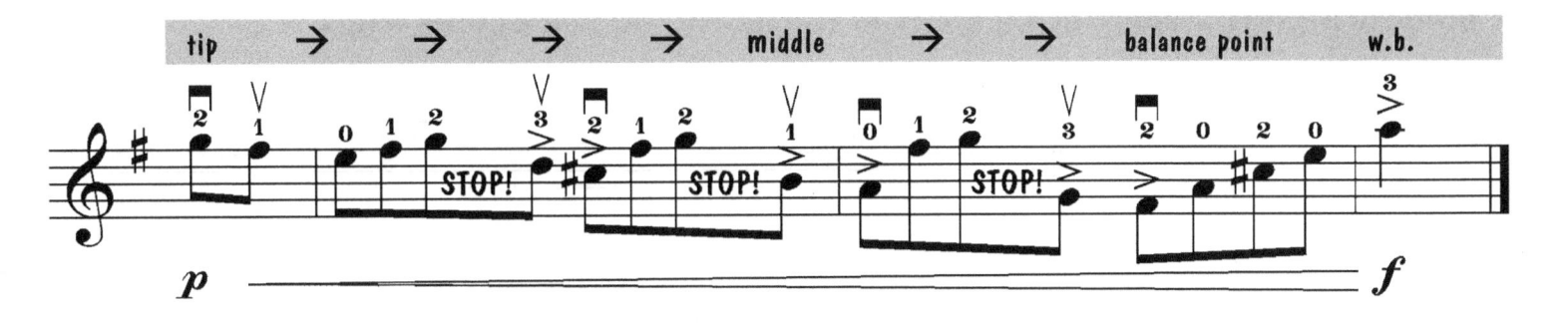

The conclusion of the 1st section with the two *raindrops*

Stress the first note, using lots of bow and energy. Pluck the two following notes with the 3rd or 4th finger of the left hand. Do you hear how lightly and softly they fade away? In the next measure, these last two notes are played with the bow. They should sound just as light and delicate as the previously plucked notes.

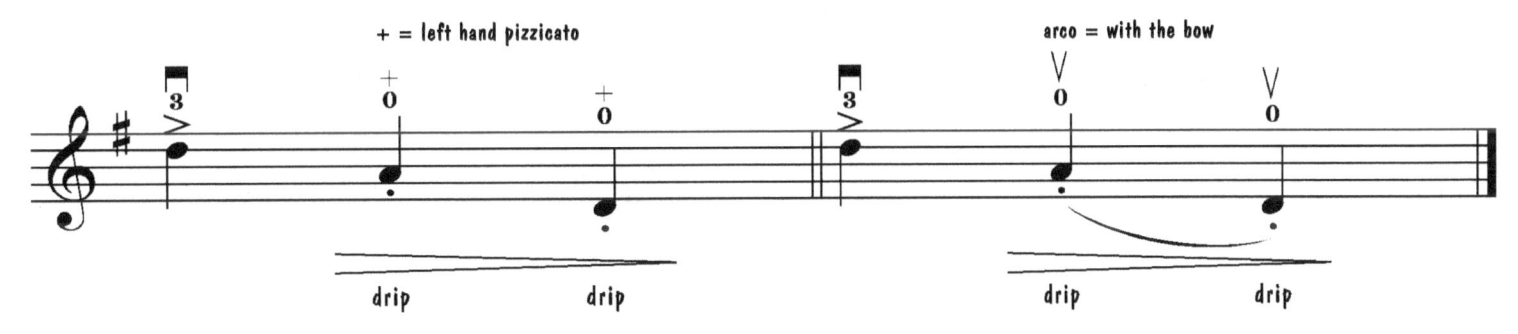

The string crossing passage and the conclusion of the 1st section

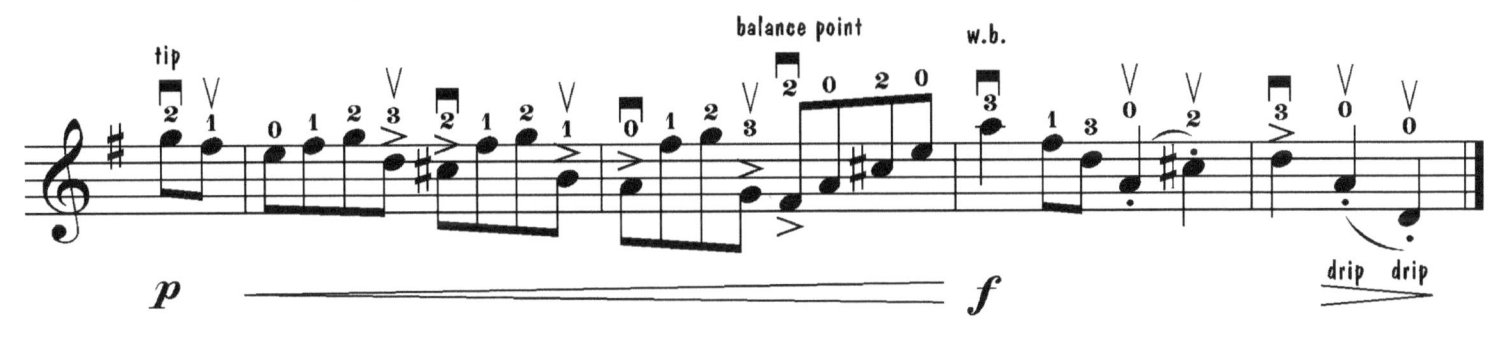

Bourrée, 1st Section – in a slow practice tempo

Double stop exercise: top - bottom - together

top bottom together   top bottom together

Place the first finger on two strings.

Review the double stop exercises on pages 24-27.

Compose a short melody using many of the newly learned double stops.

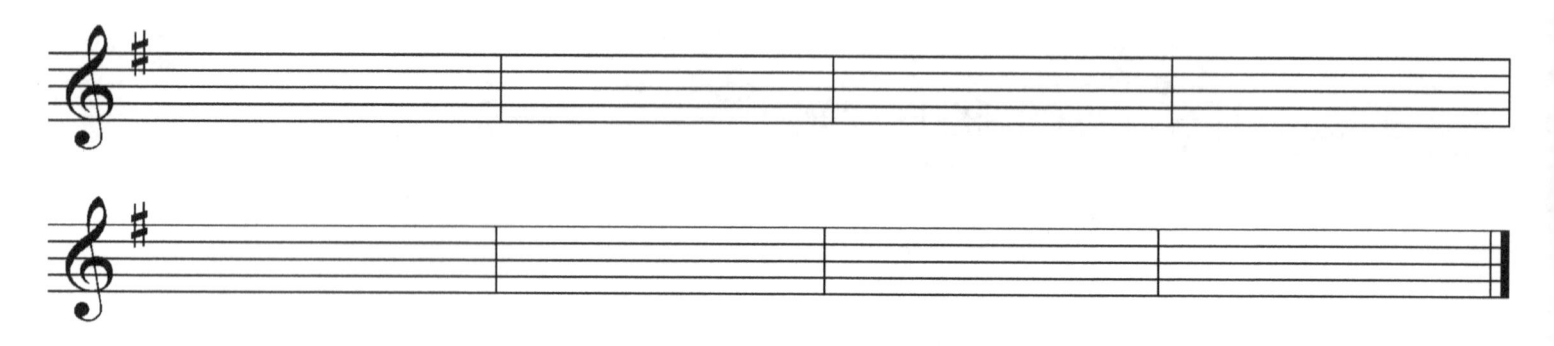

Preparatory exercise for measures 12-13

Place the high 3rd finger with the 4th finger close beside it.

The string crossing passage in the 2nd section (measures 13-16) in *piano*

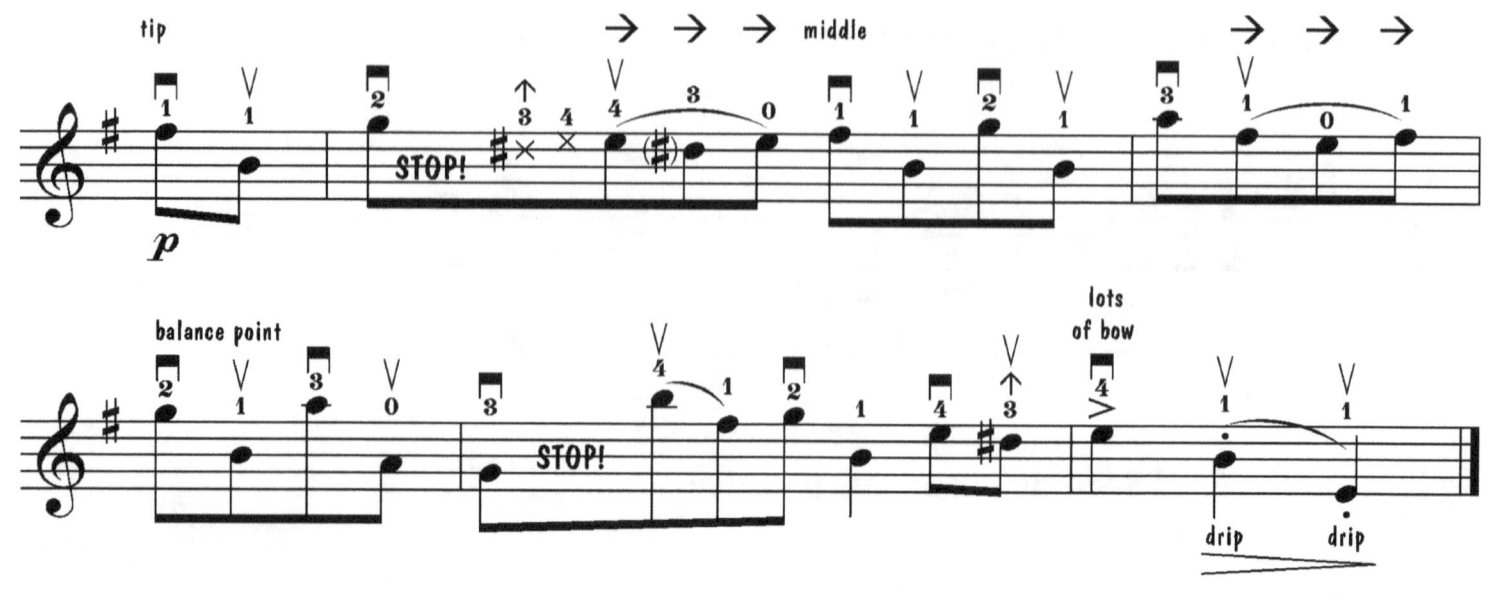

balance point

lots of bow

drip drip

42

The string crossing passage in the 2nd section (measures 13-16) in three dynamic levels

1st level = soft

Begin *piano* at the tip and bow the slur to the middle of the bow.

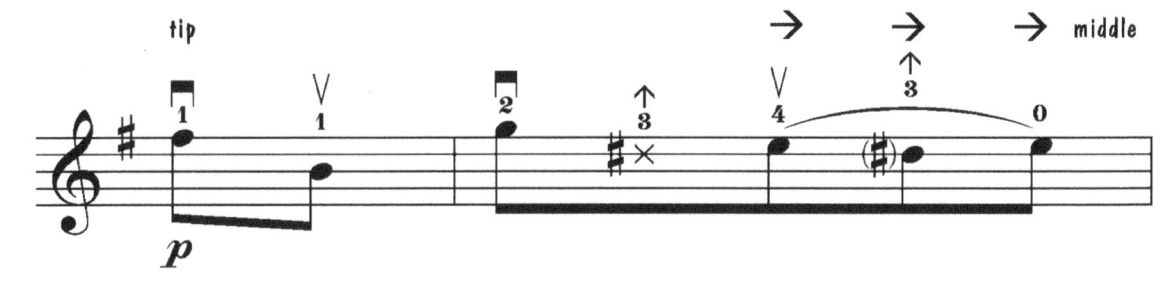

2nd level = medium loud

Did you arrive at the middle? Now play *mezzoforte* – noticeably louder – and bow the next slur to the balance point.

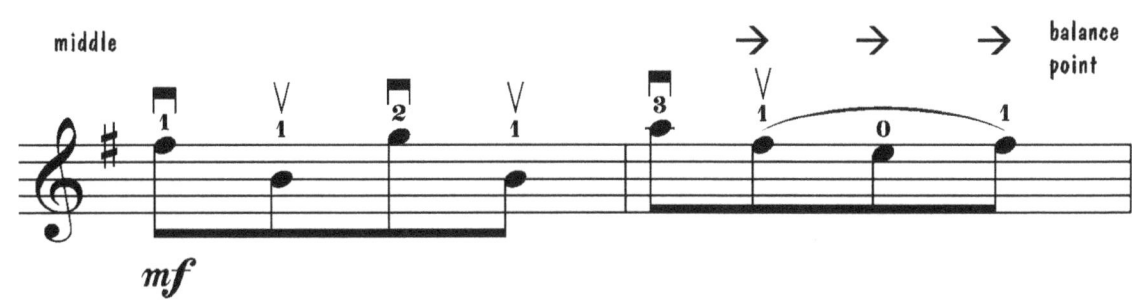

3rd level = very loud

Did you arrive at the balance point? Now you can play *forte* – even louder – and then end the passage with two gentle *raindrops*.

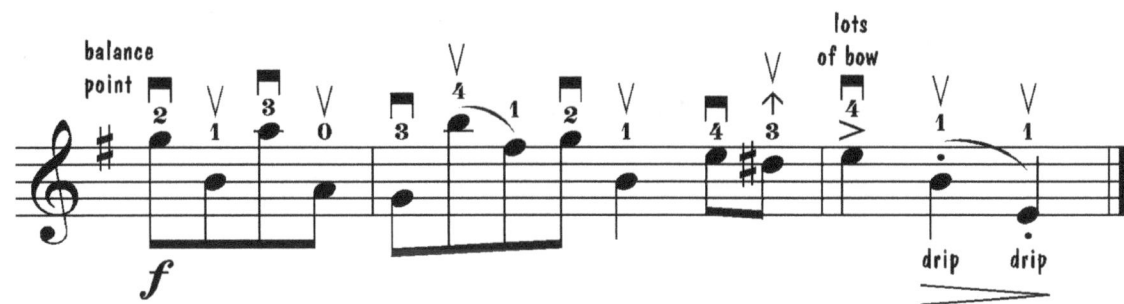

Preparatory exercise for the extended 4th finger in measure 19

a) Hold your violin like a guitar and pluck the notes. Observe how your 4th finger changes its form:

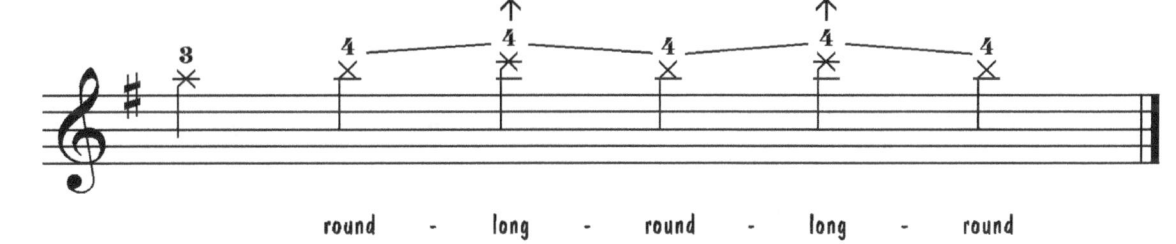

round – long – round – long – round

b) Now play the following exercise with the bow

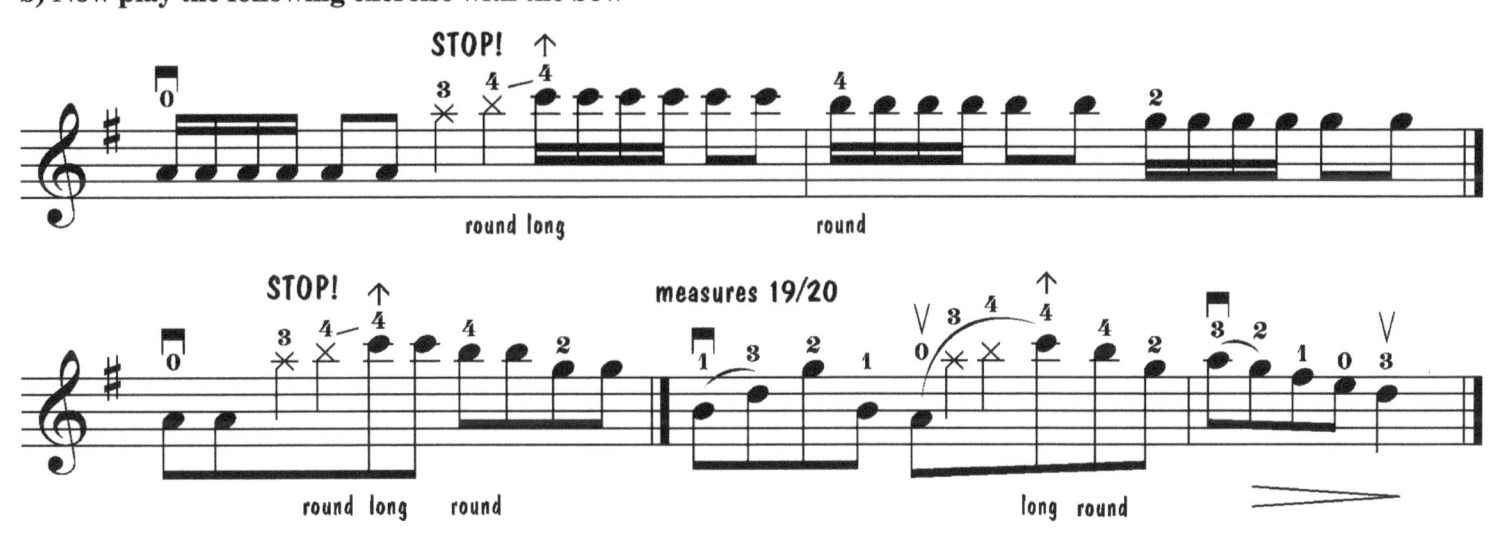

Bourrée, 2nd Section - in a slow practice tempo

46. Bourrée, 3rd Section - in a slow practice tempo
47. Bourrée, 4th Section - in a slow practice tempo

The Wandering Bow

Begin the down bow at the balance point and bow into the upper half. With every up bow, try to move slightly back towards the balance point. Make sure, though, that the up bows don't acquire an accent. Down and up bows should sound equally loud and gentle. This will certainly require lots of practice, but remember:

PRACTICE MAKES PERFECT!

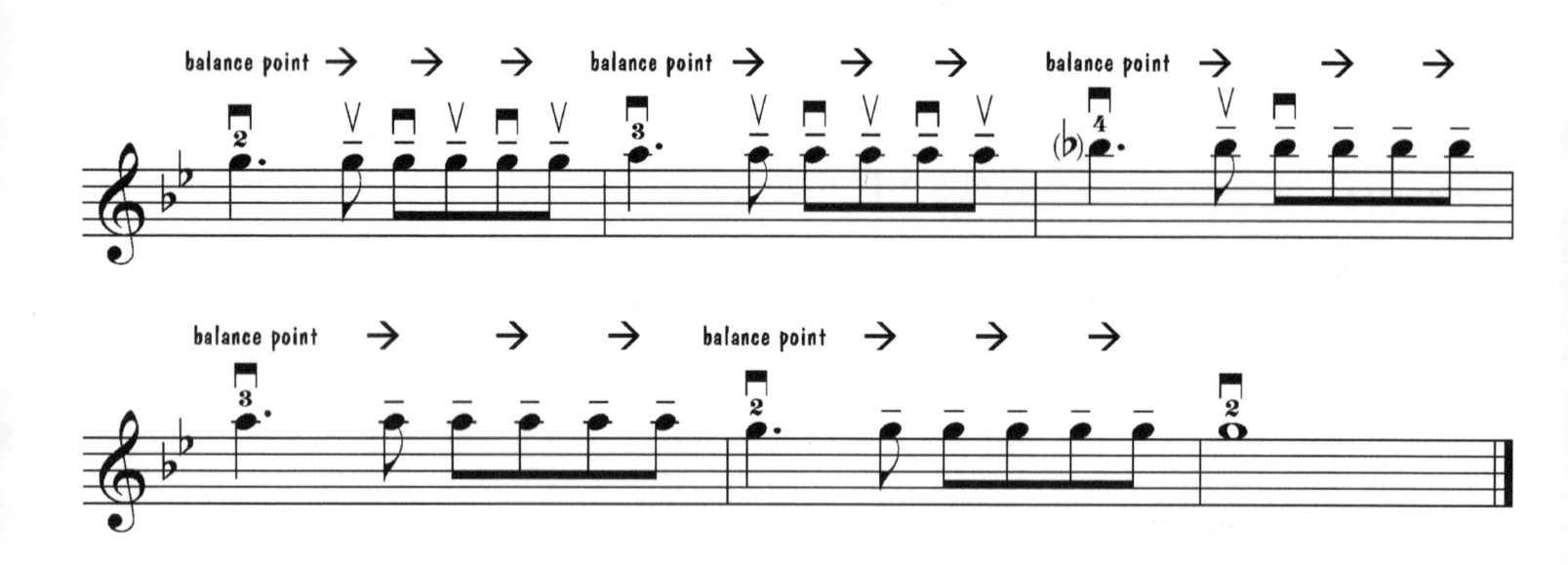

Three *wandering bow* passages in the 3rd section

The 3rd section with the *wandering bow* passages

Play tenderly and expressively with a silky tone. Be sure that even the first up-beat eighth notes sound gentle.

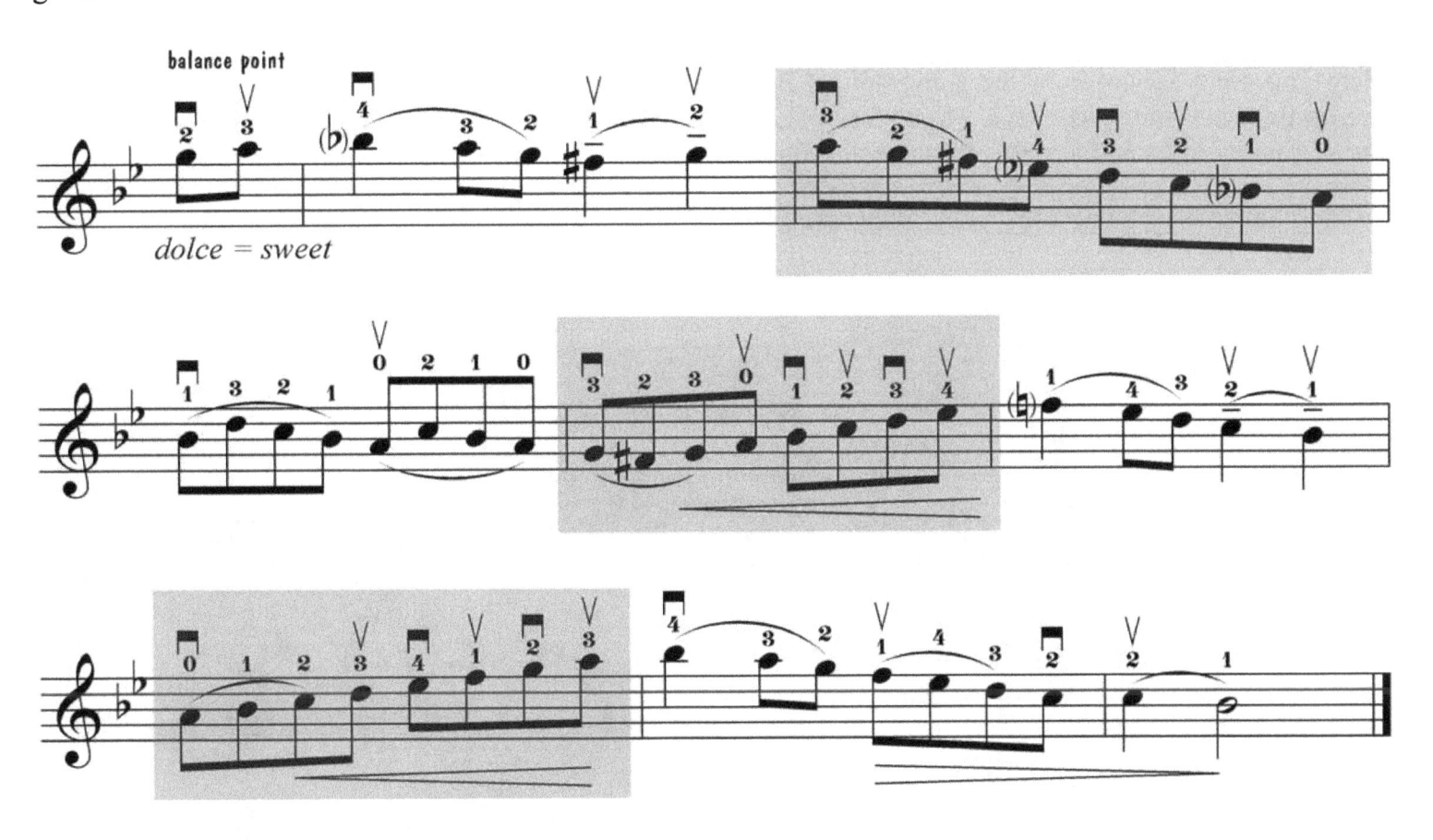

⊙ 48-51	48. Bourrée, 1st Section - in a medium practice tempo 49. Bourrée, 2nd Section - in a medium practice tempo 50. Bourrée, 3rd Section - in a medium practice tempo 51. Bourrée, 4th Section with da capo - in a medium practice tempo
⊙ 52-55	52. Bourrée, 1st Section - in performance tempo 53. Bourrée, 2nd Section - in performance tempo 54. Bourrée, 3rd Section - in performance tempo 55. Bourrée, 4th Section with da capo - in performance tempo

Congratulations!
You have reached the end of book 3B
and can look forward to many beautiful concerto movements
by Seitz, Vivaldi and Bach
awaiting you in books 4A and 4B.

The Beautiful Musical Notation of Bach's Wife, Anna Magdalena

Here you see a facsimile of the autograph of Bourrée, copied by Anna Magdalena Bach. This movement comes from the Suite No. 3 in C Major for Violoncello Solo, BWV 1009. That is why a bass clef appears at the beginning of each line rather than the familiar treble clef.

Anna Magdalena Bach helped her husband frequently and made beautiful copies of some of his works.

APPENDIX

Other Transcriptions of the Movements by *Johann Sebastian Bach*

Gavotte I and II
Bourrée

A Journey Back in Time to the World of Johann Sebastian Bach

Childhood Filled with Happiness and Sorrow (1685-1700)
Composers in Bach's Lifetime
The Clothing of the Nobles
Original Compositions and Arrangements in Baroque Music
Johann Sebastian Bach's Family Crest: Hidden Initials
A House Filled with Music (1723-1750)
My Musical Farewell

Graduation Certificate

Elementary Level

Other Transcriptions of the Movements by Johann Sebastian Bach

We have already become acquainted with the following pieces, Gavotte I and II and Bourrée, (pp. 28-29 and 38-39) in transcriptions for violin and piano as they appeared in the original Suzuki Violin School (Edition 1978). But some teachers choose to teach different versions of these pieces. For this reason, some of these versions are presented here together with the most important fundamental exercises appropriate for these transcriptions.

Gavotte I and II

30.-31. Gavotte I and II - in a medium practice tempo
32.-33. Gavotte I and II - in performance tempo

Gavotte I

Allegro

Gavotte II

Basic Exercises

Gavotte I: The two passages with the low and high first fingers

Practice all exercises on pages 30/31 and 33/34 with your teacher:

- *Gavotte II:* The bow scheme for the first phrase on the A string
- Vigorous bow strokes in the first phrase
- The second phrase: Small, delicate strokes at the balance point
- The difficult eighth-note passage with the high third finger
- The silent cradle with seven different string levels
- The change from one to two voices in four small steps

Preparatory exercise for the bow scheme in measures 26-27

Begin the first down bow at the balance point and return to the balance point with each up bow.

The same principle applies here: Begin the down bow at the balance point and return to this point with each up bow. Down and up bows should use the same amount of bow.

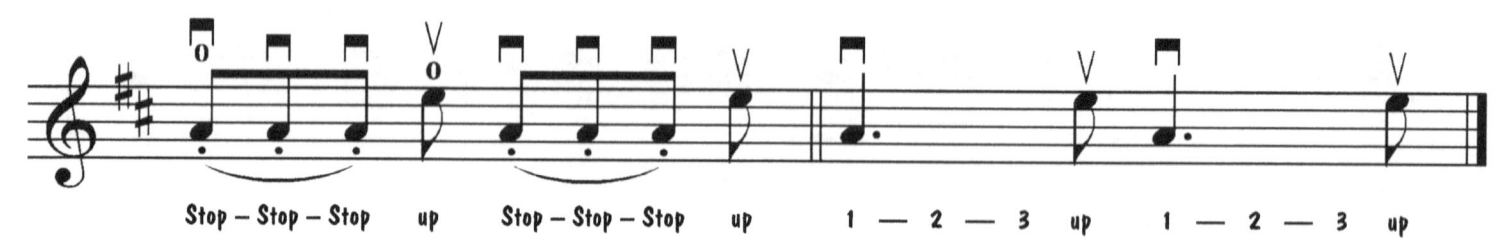

Stop – Stop – Stop   up   Stop – Stop – Stop   up   1 — 2 — 3   up   1 — 2 — 3   up

Measures 26-27, first with portato bowing and then with the slurs

Play the entire passage in the middle third of the bow.

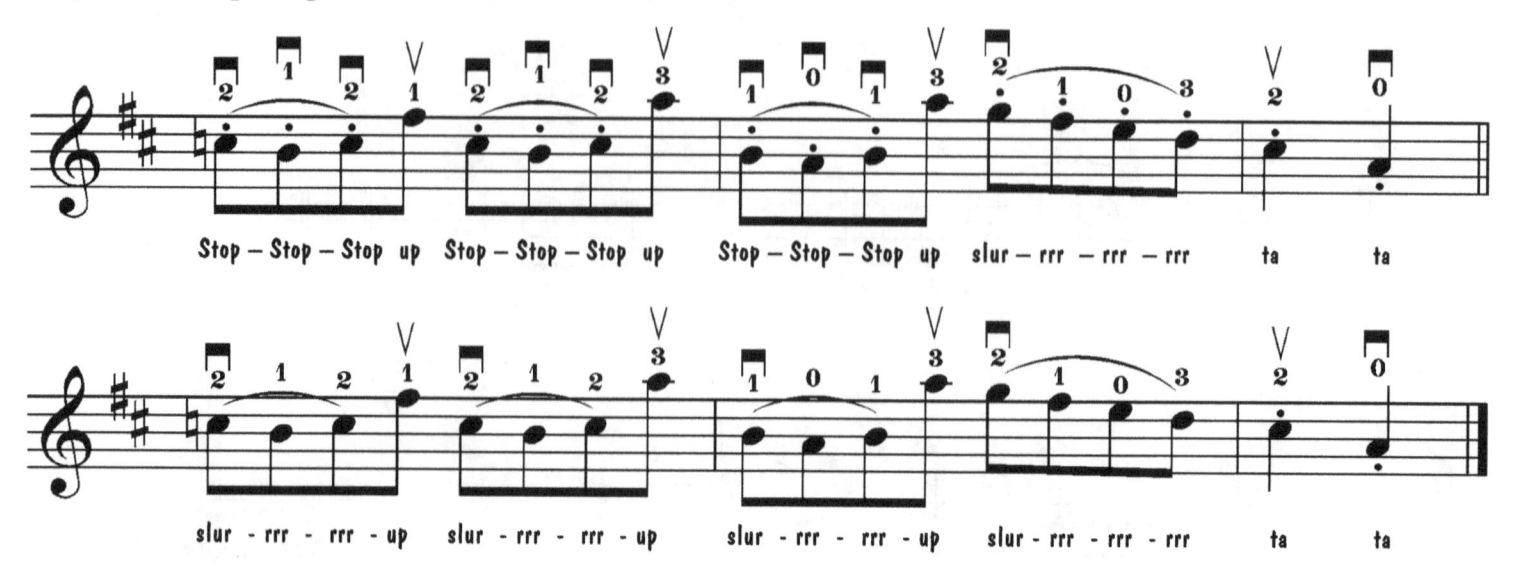

Stop – Stop – Stop up   Stop – Stop – Stop up   Stop – Stop – Stop up   slur – rrr – rrr – rrr   ta   ta

slur - rrr - rrr - up   slur - rrr - rrr - up   slur - rrr - rrr - up   slur - rrr - rrr - rrr   ta   ta

Bourrée

⊙ 56 Listen to the original version for violoncello solo.

Bourrée I

Bourrée II

dolce

D.C. Bourrée I al Fine

48. Bourrée, 1st Section – in a medium practice tempo
49. Bourrée, 2nd Section – in a medium practice tempo
50. Bourrée, 3rd Section – in a medium practice tempo
51. Bourrée, 4th Section with da capo – in a medium practice tempo

52. Bourrée, 1st Section – in performance tempo
53. Bourrée, 2nd Section – in performance tempo
54. Bourrée, 3rd Section – in performance tempo
55. Bourrée, 4th Section with da capo – in performance tempo

Basic Exercises

The beginning measures of *Bourrée*

Play energetically and let the music dance.

Come a - long, dance with me and turn 'round and 'round!

Trill exercise

Repeat the trill exercise on page 14 as well.

Preparatory exercises for the chord with the trill

little much   little much

Practice the following exercises on page 41:

- The string crossing passage (measures 5-6) with **STOP** before all string crossings to a lower string
- The conclusion of the 1st section with the two *raindrops*
- The string crossing passage and the conclusion of the 1st section

Practice the following exercises on pages 42-44:

- Double stop exercise: top - bottom - together
- Preparatory exercise for measures 12-13
- The string crossing passage in the 2nd section (measures 13-16) in *piano*
- The string crossing passage in the 2nd section (measures 13-16) in three dynamic levels
- Preparatory exercise for the extended 4th finger in measure 19
- The Wandering Bow

Three *wandering bow* passages in the 3rd section

balance point → → →   balance point → → →   balance point → → →

A Journey Back in Time to the World of Johann Sebastian Bach

I would love to put you into a time machine and program it to take you back to Germany sometime between the years of 1685 and 1750. Although no one has yet been able to invent such a wonderful machine, I still want to invite you on a short trip back in time. You will visit Johann Sebastian Bach in his world. Simply imagine that you are taking part in everything described on the following pages. You might be Sebastian's sister, making music with your younger brother. Or maybe you are one of his pupils, living in Bach's house, receiving regular lessons from him, and helping him to copy the music for his new compositions. You might even assume the role of a young court musician, or a chamber maid in Köthen castle – let your imagination run wild!

Concentrate now, I think our time machine is ready. Do you also hear the powerful voice of Johann Sebastian Bach?

Johann Sebastian Bach
in the year 1748.

Dear students, a hearty welcome to 1748!

How nice that you could come for a visit. I am now 63 years old and have been a musician my entire life. My greatest pleasure was and is to compose. I have written pieces for all possible combinations of instruments: solo instruments like the violin, cello, harpsichord or organ; chamber ensembles; orchestra; and orchestra with chorus. Up until now, more than one thousand of my compositions have been performed.

I have been told that you have also played some of my pieces. If you continue to practice diligently, you will certainly become acquainted with many more.

On the following pages, you will not only learn things about my life and music, but you can also complete interesting tasks and solve entertaining riddles.

Childhood Filled with Happiness and Sorrow (1685-1700)

Who would have thought that when I was born in the white house in Eisenach in 1685 I would one day be one of the most famous composers? Admittedly, I did grow up in a family of musicians and already as a young child demonstrated unusual interest and delight in everything musical. My father gave me my first piano and violin lessons, and even before I was old enough for school, I was allowed to listen to rehearsals and concerts and even to sit with my uncle or my elder brother, both named Johann Christoph, on the organ bench.

My elder brothers and sisters, who had long since left home, along with aunts, uncles and their children, would visit at regular intervals. We would all sing and play music until late into the night. Even as a small boy I was allowed to participate, playing my small violin in the family orchestra or singing in the family chorus. These were the most beautiful moments of my childhood.

When I was nine years old, my life changed dramatically. First, my loving mother died, followed one year later by my father. After initial uncertainties about what to do with me, my elder brothers and sisters decided that I should live with my fourteen-year elder brother, Johann Christoph. He was an organist in the Thuringian city of Ordruf and now had the additional responsibility of attending to my musical instruction, including lessons on the piano. He was a very strict teacher, for he wanted me to also have the opportunity of becoming a professional musician. With sadness, I often reflected on the lessons with my deceased father, who taught with loving insight even when my fingers flew imprecisely over the keys in wild enthusiasm. In contrast, sensing his great responsibility for my future, my elder brother would scold me when I chose to play self-composed melodies instead of the dry finger exercises he had assigned. "If you continue like this you will never become a serious musician! You will end up in the gutter! For punishment you will now play this finger exercise one hundred times in a row – and without mistakes!" This scenario recurred time and again.

Through the untimely death of my parents I had lost my ideal world. I was often very sad, though I still appreciate my brother's sacrifice today. Had he not been so supportive of me and my musical training, my life would certainly have turned out differently.

Johann Christoph had a music book filled with wonderful music that I would have loved to play. But he thought this music was much too difficult for me, so he locked the book in a cabinet. I would only be allowed to play the pieces after I acquired what he thought to be a solid technique. But I had other ideas! For six months, I managed to sneak into the music room late at night, pull the desired music carefully through the laticework of the closed cabinet with my thin fingers, and copy it by hand in the moonlight – note for note and page for page. When my brother was playing the organ in church, I would take my copied music out of its hiding place and joyfully practice these pieces. Unfortunately, Johann Christoph came home earlier than expected one day and listened with amazement as I played. He became furious at my disobedience when he saw the copy of the forbidden music. Without one word, he took the manuscripts away, and I never saw them again.

In those days, I felt very lonely and unhappy: I had lost both my parents and my home, my elder brother was almost always extremely rough on me, my beloved music was out of reach, and six months of laborious work had been for nothing...
But something valuable did remain for the rest of my life: My love of music. This helped me again and again through difficult times, opening a beautiful, inner world for me where I could forget about everything.

1ST ASSIGNMENT

In my day, there were a remarkable number of composers alive whose compositions are still commonly heard and played in your time. You have already played pieces by five of these composers, whose names can be found in the table below.

Do you know which five composers these are? Write them here:

1.
2.
3.
4.
5.

Composers Alive in Bach's time

Year	1685	1692	1706	1732	1734	1739	1741	1743	1750
Age of J.S. Bach	Born on March 21st	7 y.o.	21 y.o.	47 y.o.	49 y.o.	54 y.o.	56 y.o.	58 y.o.	Died on July 28th at the age of 65
Composers in Bach's Lifetime	Händel born on Feb. 23rd Rameau (2 y.o.) Telemann (4 y.o.) Vivaldi (7 y.o.) Corelli (32 y.o.) Lully (53 y.o.)	Tartini born on April 8th	Martini born on April 24th	Haydn born on March 31st	Gossec born on Jan. 17th	Dittersdorf born on Nov. 2nd	Grétry born on Feb. 8th	Boccherini born on Feb. 19th	Boccherini (7 y.o.) Grétry (9 y.o.) Gossec (16 y.o.) Haydn (18 y.o.) Martini (44 y.o.) Tartini (58 y.o.) Rameau (67 y.o.) Telemann (69 y.o.)

2ND ASSIGNMENT

What do a prince and princess in different costumes

have to do with a musical composition in different arrangements?

A sentence somewhere on this page will provide the answer!

Here you see my previous lord, Prince Leopold, with his wife. He was a great friend of music. This couple has changed clothes three times for you, showing three different party costumes. The nobles and their attendants usually wore long, curly wigs. These were meant to give a man a lion-like appearance. I also had to wear a wig for official occasions.

The expensive woman's apparel was tailored from velvet and silk and was decorated with fine lace. Although it was certainly beautiful to look at, it was not very comfortable to wear! A tight corset trimmed the waistline. A heavy hooped skirt, a framework made of wood and wire, came next. Over this came a valuable petticoat, and the last layer would be the stately ceremonial dress. All of these garments together often weighed more than thirty pounds!

Original Compostions and Arrangements

You probably can't imagine that in earlier times, we composers often borrowed **musical works from other composers**, adding alterations which varied from slight to extreme.

As an example, I was very fond of many concertos by Antonio Vivaldi, adapting them in many different ways. Sometimes I just changed Vivaldi's instrumentation, but other times I provided new harmonies or different bass lines and melodies.

I had just as much fun giving my **own works** a new costume. In the year 1775, my student Johann Friedrich Agricola wrote: "Bach often played the pieces for violin or violoncello solo on the clavichord adding chordal accompaniments to the melody."

Apropos, I am happy to have learned that this practice was later continued by the composers Felix Mendelssohn-Bartholdy and Robert Schumann. Both wrote piano accompaniments for my solo violin works, for which they are unfortunately criticized today by musicologists and some violin teachers.

3ʳᴅ Assignment
Johann Sebastian Bach's Family Crest

Find my initials in the family crest which I designed!

**These initials
are hidden in the family crest:**

J S B

**This is a rough sketch of how the
artistically drawn letters look:**

In the crest, the lines are not always continuous.
This makes finding them more difficult.

Assignment A: Color Bach's initials in the family crest!

Assignment B: Mirror play

Now hold a small mirror to the left or right of the my crest, angled so that you can see the crest's reflection in the mirror. The reflection looks exactly like the crest on the page before you! Try this with other pictures or symbols in this book. Do their reflections look the same as the original?

Assignment C: Make a drawing!

Now for a real challenge! Can you make a drawing where the reflection looks the same as the original?

A House Filled with Music (1723-1750)

In 1723 I took on the respected position of Thomas Cantor in Leipzig. Being responsible for the music in four Leipzig churches kept me very busy. In addition, I taught music and Latin in the famous Thomas School. Returning home, tired after completing my day's work, my wife, Anna Magdalena, my children and my students were waiting impatiently for me. Many of my students lived with us for long periods of time, expecting regular lessons from me. Sounds of various musical instruments emanated from every room in the house, even the pantry. Anna Magdalena and I listened every day - quasi in passing – whether the children were practicing carefully and correctly.

The entire household, family as well as guest students, would often sit together in the large music room at the old oak table, neatly copying the parts for my new compositions from the scores on large pages, all under the watchful eye of Anna Magdalena.

I have neglected to mention that Anna Magdalena was my second wife. Perhaps you can imagine how difficult it was for me when Maria Barbara died. Although three of our seven children had died as infants, I was suddenly left alone with four children. Through music I became acquainted with Anna Magdalena, at that time just twenty years old. She was a talented singer whom I regularly engaged for my concerts. She not only lovingly raised the children from my first marriage, but she also provided us with thirteen more children, ten of whom survived.

I love each of my surviving children dearly. Although all have mastered at least one instrument, four of my sons have even followed in my footsteps to become composers:

- Wilhelm Friedemann Bach (1710-1784)
- Carl Philipp Emanuel Bach (1714-1788)
- Johann Christoph Friedrich Bach (1732-1795)
- Johann Christian Bach (1735-1782)

My loving wife, Anna Magdalena, played piano very well when she was younger. Regretfully, her many duties as wife and mother have left hardly any time for practice. For this reason, I put together two small music books with many easy, but beautiful, pieces. There are still many empty pages, but whenever I find a suitable piece - it might even be from another composer - I copy it into one of the books. She is very fond of them, proudly shows each new piece to our children, and guards the collection like a precious treasure. By the way, Minuets 2 and 3 from your book 1B can also be found in one of the piano collections of Anna Magdalena.

My Musical Farewell

Dear students, thank you very much for your visit to my world. To conclude, I want to give you a musical farewell. Two of my friends, the cellist Michael Bach (not a relative!) and the violinist Rudolf Gähler, have agreed to play some movements from my solo violin and solo cello works for you. You will hear:

56. *Bourrée I and II* (5th movement) from the *Suite No. 3 for Violoncello Solo, BWV 1009*
57. *Gavotte en Rondeau* (3rd movement) from the *Partita in E Major for Violin Solo, BWV 1006*
58. *Preludio* (1st movement) from the *Partita in E Major for Violin Solo, BWV 1006*

On the facing page you see the first page of the *Preludio* from the *Partita in E Major for Violin Solo*, copied in my hand. I have asked my friend to play this piece in an especially swift tempo for you.

My parting assignment for you:

How far can you follow along in the music as you listen?

Dear students, if you continue to practice diligently and with delight, you just might play these pieces as well as my two friends one day.

This I wish you from my heart,

Your *Johann Sebastian Bach*

Graduation Certificate

_____
(Student's Name)

has successfully completed all fundamental technical exercises
for the elementary level (Books 1-3)
and can now proceed to the intermediate level (Books 4-7).

Date and teacher's signature

1. Tone and Vibrato exercises
    A vibrato exercise of choice   1. _____
    English Canon   2. _____
    The Bell Song   3. _____

2. Position Exercises
    Marionette Dance in 2nd position on all strings   4. _____
    Marionette Dance in 3rd position on all strings   5. _____
    Climbing Melodies in the 1st, 2nd and 3rd positions   6. _____
    Nightingale – Trill Exercise in the 1st, 2nd and 3rd Positions   7. _____

3. Exercises for the Left Hand
    Exercises with Fourths   8. _____
    The Snake Scale   9. _____

4. Bow Exercises
    Bow exercises across two strings   10. _____
    Bow exercises across three strings   11. _____

5. Double Stop and Chord Exercises
    Double stops with the melody in the upper voice   12. _____
    Double stops with the melody in the lower voice   13. _____

6. Paganini Motion   14. _____